DALLAS COWBOYS
QUIPS & QUOTES

DALLAS COWBOYS QUIPS & QUOTES

Alan Burton

State House Press

McMurry University
Abilene, Texas

Library of Congress Cataloging-in-Publication Data

Burton, Alan, 1956-
    Dallas Cowboys quips & quotes / Alan Burton.
      p. cm.
    Includes bibliographical references and index.
    ISBN-13: 978-1-933337-09-8 (pbk. : alk. paper)
    ISBN-10: 1-933337-09-5 (pbk.: alk. paper) 1. Dallas Cowboys
(Football team)—Quotations, maxims, etc. 2. Dallas Cowboys (Football
team)—Miscellanea. I. Title.

GV956.D3B87 2006
796.332'64097642812–dc22

                2006016341

State House Press
McMurry Station, Box 637
Abilene, TX 79697-0637
(325) 793-4682
www.mcwhiney.org

Printed in the United States of America

Distributed by Texas A&M University Press Consortium
www.tamu.edu/upress
1-800-826-8911

ISBN-13: 978-1-933337-09-8
ISBN-10: 1-933337-09-5
10 9 8 7 6 5 4 3 2 1

Book designed by Rosenbohm Graphic Design

Contents

Photographs used in the introduction are from the author's personal collection.

For my Dad

INTRODUCTION

For a kid growing up in small-town Texas, the early 1960s were a simple time, at least in terms of being a sports fanatic.

We're talking about Sherman, Texas, a conservative community with a population of about 20,000 at that time and located sixty miles north of Dallas near Lake Texoma and the Red River. I can only assume Sherman was a typical small Texas town during our "wonder years."

Not that we were immune to trauma—on November 22, 1963, President John F. Kennedy was assassinated while riding in a motorcade in downtown Dallas. My first grade classmates at Fairview Elementary and I weren't quite old enough to realize the impact of the tragedy, but it was indeed a sad time.

As kids, we enjoyed the simple pleasures of going to the Saturday picture show at the Texas Theatre on Houston Street, walking around downtown, and, in the summer, participating in the only game in town—boys baseball.

In the summer, we followed the exploits of Mickey Mantle and the powerful New York Yankees, who were featured frequently on TV's game of the week with broadcasters Dizzy Dean and Pee Wee Reese. We also kept an eye on that new major league team down in Houston—the Colt 45s, who evolved into the Astros and eventually wound up inhabiting the first indoor domed stadium—the Astrodome. Radio, with announcers Gene Elston, Loel Passe and Harry Kalas, was our most reliable source in tracking the many frustrations of the team.

When autumn arrived, we journeyed downtown to Bearcat Stadium on cool Friday nights to watch the Sherman Bearcats take on such arch-rivals as the Denison Yellow Jackets, Greenville Lions, Garland Owls, Mesquite Skeeters, Paris Wildcats, Richardson Eagles, and Highland Park Scots. High school football didn't get any better than that.

Saturday was reserved for the college football game of the week on TV and the Southwest Conference games on radio, courtesy of the Humble Oil-Enco-Exxon radio network. Those games were truly brought to life on our transistor radios by the vivid descriptions of such announcers as Kern Tips, Connie Alexander, and Jack Dale.

On Saturday nights, there was another high school football game in town, that being the town's pre-integration all black school—the Fred Douglass High School Panthers. Douglass played its home games in Bearcat Stadium, with both whites and blacks in attendance.

In 1964, Fred Douglass captured the Prairie View Interscholastic League state championship—the only state football title in Sherman history. That team included a future NFL lineman by the name of Vernon Holland. The Panthers' '64 season was also memorable because they downed arch-rival Denison Terrell 100-0. That's right, 100-0.

After church on Sunday, it was time for the National Football League and, specifically, the Dallas Cowboys. Long before they were "America's Team," the Cowboys were "Texas's Team," with apologies to the American Football League and the Houston Oilers.

The early-day Cowboys were, at best, mediocre. But they had neat uniforms with stars on the shoulders and played in the tradition-filled, if not fan-filled, Cotton Bowl. Over the years, the uniforms changed into a more glitzy look, and the team actually became successful.

The franchise always seemed to have more than its share of "characters" who would later be immortalized in print and at

Walt Garrison

Bob Lilly

Don Meredith

To Alan
Best Wishes
Mel Renfro
#20
Cowboys 64-77
"HOF-96"

4-12-98

Mel Renfro

the movies (i.e., "North Dallas Forty," the novel written by former Cowboys receiver Pete Gent that was later made into a movie).

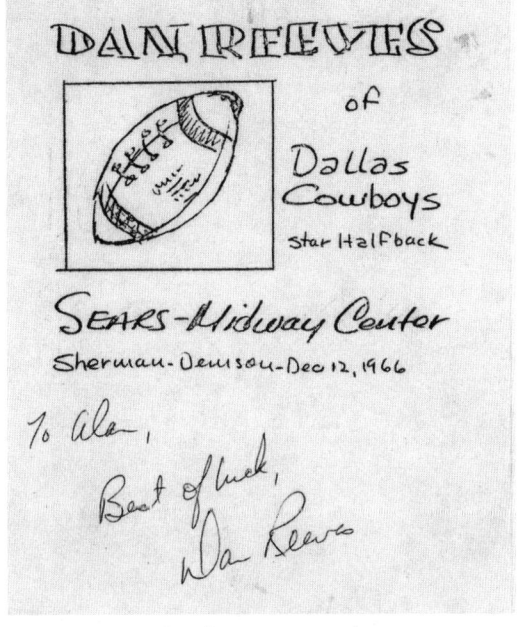

Dan Reeves autograph

Among those famous and infamous Cowboys wearing the blue and silver uniform was Dandy Don Meredith, an underrated and over-criticized quarterback who possessed both extraordinary leadership and partying abilities. He retired early after philosophical differences with stern Cowboys head coach Tom Landry. Meredith quickly re-emerged as a popular television personality, serving up humorous quips on ABC's Monday Night Football.

Other colorful Cowboys included Bob Lilly, Lee Roy Jordan, Bob Hayes ("The World's Fastest Human"), Lance Rentzel, and a couple of basketball players turned football players—defensive back Cornell Green and Gent.

My dad took us to several games at the Cotton Bowl at Fair Park in Dallas, and it was always a memorable time. Later trips to a modern Texas Stadium in Irving were never as enjoyable as those Cotton Bowl days.

And every Sunday, the "Tom Landry TV Show" appeared on Channel 4 in Dallas with Frank Glieber as host. Landry always dissected the

Jerry Tubbs

previous week's game with projector highlights and then offered up predictions of each upcoming NFL game. When it came time to pick the Cowboys' game, no matter the opponent, Landry always smirked and said, "I'll have to go with the Cowboys this week."

By virtue of living in Sherman, we were also fortunate to avoid the NFL blackout rule (which forbade local telecasts of home games) through the graces (and ingenuity) of our local TV station, KXII (Channel 12). I'm not at all sure the station was outside the legal distance to air the games, but it usually found a way to do so. We would often hear stories of rabid Dallas fans driving up to Sherman motels on Sunday afternoons just to watch the game. Later, the NFL amended the blackout rule to allow a telecast if the game was sold out seventy-two hours prior to kickoff.

Back before the days of arbitration and multi-year, multi-million dollar contracts, the Cowboys players were "real" people who held regular jobs during the off-season. Don Meredith was a stockbroker who also did weekend sportscasts on Channel 8. Tight end Frank Clarke also did weekend sports work for the same TV station. Other players sold real estate or worked in marketing positions.

Even in a small town like Sherman, various merchants would offer Cowboys players a personal appearance fee and bring them in to sign autographs (at no charge to us kids). Among the players who came were backup quarterback Jerry Rhome, running back Walt Garrison, linebacker Dave Edwards, offensive lineman Rayfield Wright, and running back Dan Reeves. It was a big deal as a store full of kids waited in eager anticipation of the "up close and personal" free autographs.

On other occasions, players ventured to our fair city for other reasons. Don Meredith once spoke at an Austin College sports banquet, while Bob Lilly offered remarks at a Sherman High School athletic banquet.

Rayfield Wright

In the early 1960s, three players—linebacker Jerry Tubbs, defensive end George Andrie, and offensive lineman Mike Connelly—appeared at a benefit basketball game at Austin College to sign autographs. I remember this appearance vividly: A group of local coaches was playing the Harlem Magicians in the exhibition contest. The Magicians, a lesser-known version of the Harlem Globetrotters, featured ex-Globetrotter Marques Haynes, reputed to be the "world's greatest dribbler."

At halftime, Tubbs-Andrie-Connelly sat side-by-side at the scorer's table as a herd of kids formed a long line. As I recall, Tubbs and Andrie had player photos to sign, but Connelly did not; instead, he had to sign the back of one of the other player's photos. I also remember thinking that Connelly must not like kids—he seemed to be scowling at us. In retrospect, I guess he wasn't too happy about not having his own photo to sign, or, well, maybe he just didn't like kids.

My other memorable autograph experience happened on December 12, 1966 (the day before my tenth birthday) at Sears in Sherman. I walked into an area between the sporting goods and, I think, the chain saw department, to find a rookie running back sitting at a table by himself. I mean all by himself. Just him and me. He seemed rather cheerful to see me as he said "hi" and handed me a paper that read, "To Alan, Best of luck, Dan Reeves."

For many pre-teenagers, it wasn't so much getting the autograph or even who it was—in fact, many times you weren't quite sure whose autograph it was you were getting. (I think I was about eight years old when I obtained the signatures of Tubbs, Connelly, and Andrie). You just knew it was somebody important and that you'd better take advantage of the opportunity. This was a far more innocent time, long before the days of sports memorabilia shows, pricey autograph fees and restrictions, and eBay internet buying/selling opportunities.

In this collection, I have attempted to replay the first forty-five years of the Dallas Cowboys in quips and quotes gathered and sifted from a variety of sources over the years (see the Bibliography for a complete list of references). Included are the words of players and coaches, for and against the Cowboys, as well as owners, writers, broadcasters, fans and other observers. To go along with the quotes, I've sprinkled in some autographs and photos from my personal collection and some fact boxes about the team's history.

I hope you have as much fun reading this stroll down memory lane as much as I have had in putting it together.

FIRST QUARTER
A Star is Born (1960s)

At the annual league meetings in Miami Beach, Florida, in 1960, Clint Murchison, Jr. and Bedford Wynne were awarded an expansion franchise in the National Football League. Thus were born the Dallas Cowboys, who were destined to forever change the course of professional football.

Tom Landry, an assistant coach with the New York Giants, and Tex Schramm were anointed as head football coach and general manager, respectively.

From humble beginnings, the Cowboys slowly, but surely, built themselves into a league power by the time the NFL and AFL (American Football League) merged at the end of the decade.

The image of Dallas, and even the Cowboys, was dealt a heavy blow on Nov. 22, 1963, when President John F. Kennedy was assassinated in downtown Dallas. It would be many years before the country would "forgive" the city for this tragedy, and the Cowboys would eventually play a critical role in shaping a more positive image for "Big D."

In the early years, playing before sparse crowds in the Cotton Bowl, the team struggled. Through its first five seasons, Dallas managed an embarrassing won-loss-tied record of 18-46-4. The corner was turned in 1965, as Landry, armed with a 10-year contract

Game program for the first of two NFL championship games that Dallas and Green Bay played in 1967, the first on January 1 in Dallas and the famous 'Ice Bowl' in Green Bay on December 31.

extension, led the Cowboys to a 7-7 record and a berth in the NFL Playoff Bowl Game.

The next two seasons would see Landry's team advance to the NFL title games, only to lose both to the Green Bay Packers in the same year, 1967, on January 1 in Dallas and on December 31 in Green Bay.

The 1967 "Ice Bowl" championship game in Green Bay on December 31 was arguably the most famous title bout in league history, with Green Bay scoring in the last seconds to claim a 21-17 win in Wisconsin's thirteen-degree-below-zero weather.

The Cowboys were beginning to capture the hearts of America, not only with their innovative offense (multiple sets) and defense ("Flex," later known as "Doomsday defense"), but with their colorful individuals. There was the stoic and impeccably dressed Tom Landry walking the sidelines, never showing any emotion. There was happy-go-lucky quarterback "Dandy Don" Meredith. "Bullet Bob Hayes," the world's fastest human. Bob Lilly. Lee Roy Jordan. Chuck Howley. Mel Renfro. Cornell Green.

Don Perkins. Lance Rentzel. Walt Garrison. George Andrie. Pete Gent. And the list goes on.

After the two near-misses against Green Bay, the 1968 season ended for Dallas with a disappointing loss to Cleveland's Browns in the Eastern Championship game.

In the summer of 1969, both Meredith and Perkins decided to call it quits. And once again the Cowboys would endure frustration, losing to Cleveland in the '69 Eastern Championship game. Dallas had come so far, but was now tagged as "Next Year's Champions" —a team that couldn't win the big game.

It was the end of a grand era in Cowboys history, but an ever grander one was on the horizon.

* * *

"You could make more money investing in government bonds, but football is more fun."

– Dallas Cowboys owner Clint Murchison

"I named the team. I did the logo and picked the colors. Before we got the franchise, we planned to name the team the Dallas Steers. But after thinking about it, nobody liked the idea of a castrated bull. So we decided to name them the Dallas Rangers. Rangers was a good name; it embodied the state. But then there was a professional baseball team calling itself the Dallas Rangers. Clint was leaving for vacation in the Bahamas. He said, 'Well, you make this decision.' So he took off, and I named them the Cowboys."

– Dallas Cowboys President-General Manager Tex Schramm

"You had a mixture of young players who really didn't have much potential and older players who were on their last legs or were a little hard to manage."
    – Tom Landry, on his first year of coaching the Cowboys

"(Bob) Lilly is a big disappointment. I'll be surprised if he ever plays pro football."
    – College All-Star coach Otto Graham on the Cowboys defensive lineman and number one draft pick, 1961

"I had a little bit of a dream what professional sports would be like. I'd watched the New York Yankees baseball team, seen on TV and in pictures in the papers how nice their locker room was. Then I went to my first Cowboys practice at Burnet Field in Dallas, which was a condemned baseball field over in Oak Cliff. I couldn't believe it. This was the NFL?"
    – Bob Lilly

"When I was weighed, I used to put two five-pound weights in the waistband of my jock. The needle hit 240, and Jim Myers, the Cowboys line coach, would say, 'You don't look that heavy. I guess you've just got a real solid build.'"
    – Dallas Cowboys center Mike Connelly

"We felt like we were some real hated bastards. The sentiment was that Dallas had killed the president. It wasn't a good time to be a Dallas Cowboy . . . We felt the whole country indicting us."
    – Dallas Cowboys fullback Don Perkins, after the assassination
      of President Kennedy in Dallas, 1963

"We were really kind of worried about getting killed. We stood there going, 'I wonder if there are any snipers around here?' We

wore our helmets the whole time and wore those big parkas."
   – Bob Lilly, on playing in Cleveland days after the assassination

"I think the assassination affected the Cowboys for at least another year, as far as feeling guilty about our city. A little ashamed. Dallas was kind of a coming star and then all of a sudden it was tarnished. It took Dallas a long time to get over it. It didn't take the team quite as long. Meredith and I, as Texans, probably felt it a little more. Coach Landry, too. We were kind of ashamed of our city. It's not the best mentality for playing football. Somehow, emotionally, it did something."
   – Bob Lilly

"I liked Green Bay's uniform, with the gold pants. Then I saw Georgia Tech. They also had gold pants, but they had a real good-looking white jersey with the numbers on top of the shoulder pads rather than on the arms. I thought that look was terrific. I copied Georgia Tech for the Cowboy uniform."
   – Tex Schramm on the Cowboys' new uniforms in 1964

"The metallic color was a new color. The manufacturers had to make a new dye with new materials. It was a unique color that became associated with the Cowboys. The new uniform was a big deal in the image and popularity of the Cowboys; it was classy and original and people loved it."
   – Tex Schramm on the new metallic silver pants

"He just started to cry, and nobody knew what to do. But we saw the real man that day. He was crying because he felt he had let us down. We never forgot that moment. It was the turning point for the Dallas Cowboys."
   – Bob Lilly, on Tom Landry's locker room emotion after a fifth
      straight loss in 1965

"This is our biggest moment because it is the first time we've reached the level of excellence. No matter what happens from here on out, it's something we'll always remember."
   – Tex Schramm, after Dallas beat the Giants to qualify for the NFL Playoff Bowl

"It was a team effort."
   – Tom Landry, after Dallas was thrashed in the NFL Playoff Bowl by Baltimore, 35-3

"When they started winning in '66 it was incredible, like the Beatles or something. I remember one time we landed at Love Field after a big road win and the fans knocked down the fence and surrounded the airplane. We all ducked our heads and went out the back door. I was hiding behind the linemen. People were just going crazy. Things were never the same with the Cowboys after that year. They were really, really big."
   – Former Dallas Cowboys radio play-by-play announcer Bill Mercer

"We captured people's imagination because we had good-looking uniforms with that star on the helmet. We had a modest head coach that people respected. We had a snappy quarterback. We had track men playing defensive back. We were just the underdog that people would be attracted to."
   – Tex Schramm

"Everyone says there are some things in your life you never forget, and one was when our president was shot, and another was the Ice Bowl. I may have forgotten a lot of other things, but I will never forget the Ice Bowl."
   – Bob Lilly

"The Ice Bowl is what started the great popularity of the Cowboys nationwide. We were the underdog expansion team with the finger-snapping quarterback. We had a unique team. Cornell Green was a basketball player. Hayes was a track man, Reeves was a very unusual player. They were all very colorful, and they were going against mighty legends, up there fighting in those horrible conditions. We lost the game, but I think we got more out of it than the Packers in terms of image and popularity."

– Tex Schramm

Cowboys in the NFL Hall of Fame

Troy Aikman, quarterback, 1989-2000
Tony Dorsett, running back, 1977-87
Tom Landry, coach, 1960-88
Bob Lilly, defensive tackle, 1961-74
Mel Renfro, defensive back, 1964-77
Tex Schramm, president/general manager, 1959-89
Roger Staubach, quarterback, 1969-79
Randy White, defensive tackle, 1975-88
Rayfield Wright, offensive tackle, 1967-79

"The Ice Bowl was our worst loss ever. We were the better team and we were ahead, and to lose in those circumstances was just a crushing thing. We suffered for a year or two after that. I don't give a damn what anyone else says, it took us at least a year to get over it. There was a hangover. A bad hangover."

– Dallas Cowboys defensive end George Andrie

"The Cowboys were the better team, but if you lose the game, you're still the loser. The Packers drove sixty-eight yards on an icy field, and they drove a stake into the Cowboys' hearts. That game

ended a phase of the Cowboys' history. They weren't the same after that for a few years."
  – Bob Ryan of NFL Films

"We have twelve Texans on this team. They were hand-picked because they're tough. They grow them tough in Texas. We like tough football players."
  – Green Bay Packers coach Vince Lombardi after his team beat Dallas in the NFL Championship game (Ice Bowl), 1967

"If we had won that (Ice Bowl) game, see, it would have changed the whole psyche of the team . . . People started writing, started saying, that we couldn't win the big games, and right after that second Packer game, we really bombed in two games against Cleveland (1968 and 1969 conference title games) . . . we really bombed."
  – Tom Landry, 1990

"Good morning, it's sunny and seventeen degrees below zero."
– Motel telephone operator to Dallas Cowboys players the morning of the 1967 NFL title game in Green Bay, Wisconsin

"We played with great emotion as the underdogs in '66 and '67, but after that we were the team that was expected to win, and I'm not sure we were mature enough to handle that. We had a talented team, but it was a strange team in some ways, with basketball players and track stars and unusual talents, and all sorts of makeshift people plugged in. We were somewhat immature, lacking in experience, and, in my mind, lacking the talent to be a dom-

inating team. We could almost get there, but we weren't good enough to take that final step. And then we got in that mentality. Those were tough days."
– Tex Schramm

"Failure, like success, has a carryover effect. After we lost (the Ice Bowl) our chances of winning (in Cleveland in '68) were much worse. And after that loss we were at a big psychological disadvantage in the ('69) playoffs and lost again. Football is a mental game and a cycle like that is hard to break."
– Tom Landry, 1997

"We didn't prepare well for Cleveland. We worked hard, but you could sense something wasn't there. They had something we didn't and I still don't know what it was . . . It wasn't the coaches. It wasn't the money. Either we were tired or we've got losers. I don't know. I hope we have a lot of winners. Only in time will we know."
– Bob Lilly, after the playoff loss to Cleveland in 1968

"Those were the most miserable, toughest coaching years I had. When you take a good team demoralized by defeat in big games and have to turn it around. It's the toughest coaching job you can face."
– Tom Landry

"We had everything we needed to win it all, but we lacked one ingredient—a fierceness on the field. We needed to punish the opposing team, especially the backs and ends, but we didn't."
– Bob Lilly

"I guarantee you, the guys who have been on this club awhile are tired of hearing and reading how the Dallas Cowboys have so many great athletes, so much finesse, so much imagination, so

much speed. That's true, perhaps, but we'll be a lot more interested in hearing and reading it when we've won the Super Bowl."
– Bob Lilly

Don Meredith's TV Career

Following retirement, personable Dallas Cowboys quarterback Don Meredith enjoyed a successful career as a broadcaster on ABC's Monday Night Football, as a semi-regular on the "Police Story" TV series, and as a commercial spokesman for Lipton Tea.

Meredith also appeared as a guest on at least two popular TV game shows:

"Match Game," hosted by Gene Rayburn. Meredith appeared with Bart Starr on April 22-26, 1968; with Joe Garagiola on April 28-May 2, 1969; and with Burt Reynolds on Sept. 15-19, 1969

"What's My Line." On July 31, 1969, Meredith appeared as the mystery guest. Panelists were Phyllis Newman, Gene Rayburn, Jayne Meadows, and Bennett Cerf

---

"The Cowboys were a real smart team and always tough to beat, but they were a finesse team, and that's why the real aggressive, physical teams could beat them. The Packers got their nature from Lombardi and the Cowboys took their lead from Landry. He wasn't a mean coach. He was a great coach and he had a system, but he was a dapper guy and the team reflected him."
– Former NFL linebacker Sam Huff

"It is designed to stop every play on the line of scrimmage. This is the theory, you have to remember, not necessarily the result."
– Tom Landry on his Flex defense

"Gosh, I don't know how many times we were criticized for not being aggressive on defense . . . The flex gave us the undeserved reputation of not being tough, but we cut down on aggression and wanted more movement, more intelligence, more formation recognition."
– Tom Landry, 1990

"By the time you learn the flex, it's time to retire."
– Bob Lilly

"It will go down in history that Landry changed football. Before him, football was pretty straightforward. You just tried to beat the guy in front of you. Landry created the scheme defense and wide-open offense everyone adopted . . . We had some great players, but also some average players that Landry took and plugged in and made great. It was his coaching that made the difference. We got good when we started to believe in his concepts and play them well."
– Former Dallas defensive back Mike Gaechter, 1997

"Don't bother reading it, kid. Everybody gets killed in the end."
– Dallas Cowboys receiver Pete Gent, advising a rookie not to read Landry's playbook

"Better football through chemistry, huh?"
– Actor Nick Nolte, getting a pain-killing shot in the knee in order to play his wide receiver position in the movie "North Dallas Forty"

"It's like a beauty contest. It's easy to pick out the top one, two or three girls. But then the rest of them look the same."
 – Dallas Cowboys player personnel director Gil Brandt on the college draft

"I'll say one thing for them—they never try to sell you their brother-in-law as a prospect."
 – Gil Brandt on the use of computers in drafting players

"I didn't know what a free agent was until I got my first pay-check."
 – Pete Gent

Reporter: "What would have happened if the press box blew up?"
Tom Landry: "We would have had a thirty-second silent prayer and then played on. With enthusiasm."
 – Tom Landry, joking when asked after a game about a bomb threat that had been called into the press box

"I love it. It's just like the movies. At first I got so excited that I squealed and screamed. It affected my voice. Now I jump up and down and limit myself to applauding."
 – Actress Joey Heatherton and wife of Dallas receiver Lance Rentzel, on her new love of football

"If he was as big as (Dick) Butkus, he'd be illegal."
 – Dallas defensive line coach Ernie Stautner on Cowboys mid-dle linebacker Lee Roy Jordan

"To me, a football game is like a day off. I grew up picking cotton on my daddy's farm, and nobody asked for your autograph or put your name in the paper."
    –Dallas Cowboys linebacker Lee Roy Jordan

"Bob Hayes had just two speeds, and his downshift was too great when he was making his cut. He gave himself away a lot of the time."
    – Dallas Cowboys defensive back Charlie Waters

"What Bob Hayes did was change man-to-man coverage. He set up zones. And that was eventually Bob's downfall, because he failed, really, to adjust to zones."
    – Tom Landry

"If you needed four yards, you could give the ball to Walt and he'd get you four yards. If you needed twenty yards, you could give the ball to Walt and he'd get you four yards."
    – Dallas Cowboys quarterback Don Meredith on fullback
      Walt Garrison

"I landed right on my head each time and that was a good thing or I might have been hurt seriously."
    – Lance Rentzel, on being knocked out twice in a game
      against the Houston Oilers

Tom Landry: "Pete, you'll be moving to the other side this week. So get ready."
Pete Gent: "You mean, coach, that I'm going to play for Philadelphia?"
    – Cowboys receiver Pete Gent, when told he was moving from
      flanker to split end

". . . That cat is a good coach and a good man."
– Bob Hayes on Tom Landry

"Tom (Landry) is the most single-purpose, single-minded individual I've ever known. It's like a total commitment, a total dedication to a profession. I think the fact that it did not necessarily parallel mine caused more conflict with us than anything else."
– Don Meredith

"If Bud Grant and Tom Landry were in a personality contest, it would be a 0-0 draw."
– Don Meredith

"He (Don Meredith) was a great leader. Don also was probably the toughest quarterback I had. He would get off a hospital bed to play a game . . . Don was a guy who tried to cure his nervousness and ability to achieve with a happy-go-lucky attitude."
– Tom Landry

"I'd say the most important thing a quarterback can do is have his nerve endings removed. Hey, those are big people hitting you, and they hurt."
– Don Meredith

"Well, we know we'll never make Don Meredith into Bart Starr. They're different personalities. . . . Meredith is like a Babe Ruth or a Bobby Layne. If Starr is Stan Musial, Meredith is Mickey Mantle. I understand that, but sometimes I get annoyed at his flippancy."
– Tex Schramm, 1968

"He has this charisma about him. He's like Bobby Layne, a great player and leader, but an exciting person just to be around. Meredith, to me, is what I want—and what I expect—an NFL quarterback to be."
 – Los Angeles Rams defensive lineman Merlin Olsen

"If Meredith had led us over a cliff, I would have been the first one to follow. He was that great a leader. All the guys liked him and wanted to play for him . . . He just had an incredible way of motivating people."
 – Former Dallas Cowboys offensive lineman Jim Boeke, 1997

"He (Don Meredith) has leadership qualities you may find one in 10 million men. People get a kick out of being around him."
 – Dallas Cowboys offensive tackle Ralph Neely, 1968

"Men, we're in a shitload of trouble!"
 – Don Meredith, to his teammates in the huddle after they fell behind 14-0 to Green Bay in the 1966 title game

"Outlined against a gray November sky, the Four Horsemen rode again. You know them: Pestilence, Famine, Death and Meredith."
 – Dallas sportswriter Gary Cartwright's lead to a story in which Cowboys quarterback Don Meredith threw a critical interception in the fourth quarter of a 24-17 loss to Cleveland

"In critical moments, Meredith is hampered by a death-wish syndrome. Subconsciously, or perhaps at a shallow level of his conscious, he considers himself unworthy of being the best, being a championship quarterback."
 – Dr. John Gunn, a Dallas Cowboys team physician

"As far as reading defenses and knowing the game plan and what was going on, he was the best quarterback the Cowboys ever had. He could pick a defense apart . . . People never realized what a great athlete Meredith was. He was a single-digit handicap golfer. He'd kick your ass playing ping-pong or pool."
– Former Cowboys fullback Walt Garrison

"He is still one of the most amazing guys I have ever seen on any field or floor anywhere. He wasn't physically endowed like (Troy) Aikman and he didn't have an exceptional arm and he was erratic, but he had the amazing ability to coalesce everyone around him. Everyone loved him and wanted to win for him."
– Pete Gent on Meredith, 1997

"Meredith had more fun playing the game than anyone I ever saw, and it made it fun for the rest of us."
– Former Dallas Cowboys running back
Dan Reeves

"Don was a great football player who took the punishment to build Dallas to a winning team . . . Don Meredith would have taken Dallas to some Super Bowl victories in the 1970s. Don Meredith was a very good quarterback, and he had the confidence of the team."
– Dallas Cowboys quarterback Roger Staubach

"I believe you have to pay a tremendous price to be a quarterback in this league, a tremendous price. You have to be very disciplined, you have to work and perform the way Roger (Staubach) did. So that was my problem with Don . . . He just didn't see it that

way . . . We differed in the discipline I required in our system, Don didn't want that. I mean, he wanted a good time, lots of fun, but the guy played extremely well for me. He was a talented quarter-back and I'm sorry he retired so soon. I really am."
  – Tom Landry, 1990

"Tom Landry's whole theory, on the other hand, was industrial. Football was a machine with replaceable parts. This came as a result of his experiences as a bomber pilot, I presume. He didn't want to know the gunners. He didn't want to know them, because they were probably going to get killed. It was the biggest struggle between Landry and Meredith . . . Landry didn't like Meredith's lifestyle. Meredith would walk out onto the field and he wouldn't be serious enough for Landry. But that whole style that Meredith had adapted was designed to take pressure off the players and keep them believing that if Don was happy and feeling good, then we must be okay."
  – Pete Gent

"I think if Don had played for another team, for another coach, he would never have retired as early as he did. I mean, he was only thirty-one, and he was going to improve and become a great, great quarterback. I think Tom took all the joy out of football for him. He just couldn't play for Tom."
  – Lee Roy Jordan

"The time I spent with the Cowboys wasn't much fun, and my relationship with Coach Landry wasn't particularly good, and I wouldn't want to say bad things about anybody or any place but I don't want to be a hypocrite and say good things that I don't mean, so I think I'd just rather not do this, Dave."
  – Don Meredith to author Dave Klein, when asked for an inter-
    view to review his career, 1990

"Craig Morton, like Don Meredith before him, was a party animal. In fact, he was the whole zoo. Morton was like Meredith. Football was not his whole life. He was more dedicated than Meredith but that wasn't saying a lot. Craig was famous for his partying. That boy could rock and roll, let me tell you. But hell, he didn't have a wife or family and he was the quarterback for the Dallas Cowboys, which was glamorous as hell and he had a big contract, so why not enjoy it? . . . Morton proved he was a great athlete. You'd have to be great to stay out as many nights as he did and do all the crazy stuff he did and still make practice. The guy was phenomenal."
– Walt Garrison

"They all wanted another Doak Walker. To my mind, Doak Walker was at one place and the rest of us were at another. They were expecting me to be something I could never be."
– Dallas Cowboys quarterback Don Meredith, reflecting on the pressure while he was at SMU

"Once, I was sitting on this plane and just decided I didn't want to play football anymore . . . I can't explain why. I just knew it was time to quit. The same thing happened when I left 'Monday Night Football.' I just knew it was time."
– Don Meredith

"To me, Landry's low point was after that playoff loss to Cleveland my rookie year in 1969. We were getting ready to board a flight to Miami for the Playoff Bowl. People were crying for his scalp and he looked like a beaten man that day. We had a meeting at Love Field before taking off, and he was the lowest I've ever seen him. He was ashen. He'd had it and he was down."
– Roger Staubach

SECOND QUARTER
America's Team (1970s)

Dallas shook off the image of not being able to win the big game, partially at least, in 1970.

The Cowboys captured their first-ever National Football Conference crown by beating the San Francisco 49ers. The old demons re-emerged in Super Bowl V, however, as the Cowboys lost a mistake-filled 16-13 decision to the Baltimore Colts on January 17, 1971.

That bitter memory would be erased the following season, as quarterback Roger Staubach ("Captain America") and moody and silent running back Duane Thomas led Dallas to a 24-3 triumph over the Miami Dolphins in Super Bowl VI on January 16, 1972.

That 1971 season was also the year the Cowboys moved from the Cotton Bowl into the plush new confines of Texas Stadium in Irving.

The remainder of the 1970s were mostly good times for Landry's teams. The Cowboys' record-breaking streak of eight straight years in the NFL playoffs was broken in 1974 with an 8-6 record. But the club rebounded in 1975 to win the NFC title, before losing to the Pittsburgh Steelers in Super Bowl X.

Dallas claimed its second world championship on January 15, 1978, with a 27-10 triumph over the Denver Broncos in Super Bowl

XII. The following year saw Dallas advance again to the championship game, losing Super Bowl XIII once again to the Steelers.

The Cowboys ended the decade with fourteen straight winning seasons. The team's glamour and success caused Bob Ryan, an NFL Films editor, to dub them as "America's Team," a moniker despised by many of the Cowboys' opponents.

Adding to the team's mass appeal were such colorful players as Staubach, running backs Calvin Hill and Tony Dorsett, receivers Drew Pearson, Tony Hill, and Butch Johnson, defensive linemen Harvey Martin and Randy "Manster" White, defensive backs Charlie Waters and Cliff Harris, and, of course, unforgettable linebacker Thomas "Hollywood" Henderson.

After a brilliant career, Staubach retired following the '79 season.

As a new decade approached, the "times, they were a-changin'" in Big D.

* * *

"His (Tom Landry) job was never in jeopardy and will never be as long as I have control or as long as Clint Murchison is the owner of the club . . . We couldn't have a better man for the job."
– Dallas Cowboys general manager Tex Schramm, when asked if Landry's job was in danger after the team started 5-4 in 1970

"Clint (Murchison) was the perfect owner. He let the football people do their job, left them alone, didn't interfere, paid all the bills and said yes every time Schramm or Coach Landry said something had to be purchased, or some player had to be signed. He was perfect."
– Former Dallas Cowboys publicist Doug Todd

"This is not the team I used to know. . . . You ain't getting me out there."
– Retired Dallas quarterback turned Monday Night Football broadcaster Don Meredith, responding to chants of "We want Dandy" during a televised 38-0 Dallas loss to St. Louis in the Cotton Bowl, 1970

"To lose that game like we did, that was the lowest point of my career. The Ice Bowl, the Cleveland games, they were bad. But the Baltimore game was the worst I ever felt. Baltimore still doesn't impress me that much. I still feel like we had the better team. I think we kind of got screwed. I don't want to take anything away from the Colts. But we should have won. When we didn't, after we had blown so many chances, we just didn't know if we'd get another chance."
– Bob Lilly, after the team's 16-13 loss to the Baltimore Colts in Super Bowl V. Several controversial calls went against the Cowboys, and after the game, Lilly hurled his helmet in disgust fifty yards downfield

"If (Craig) Morton was a pitcher in baseball, he would have been knocked out in the first inning. He overthrew Duane (Thomas) on one wide-open touchdown and missed a lot of passes. Landry wouldn't put Staubach in. Morton played worse that day than any quarterback I'd ever seen in a big game, but Landry was set in his ways and stubborn enough not to make a change."
– Cowboys defensive back Herb Adderley on the Super Bowl loss to Baltimore

Dallas mayor Erik Jonsson: "If you take the Cowboys out of (the Cotton Bowl), what are you suggesting we put there instead?"
Cowboys owner Clint Murchison: "What about an electronics plant?"

"It will be the finest football facility in the United States. I think everybody will eventually realize the benefits from Texas Stadium and feel that one of these days we'll have the Super Bowl there."
– Tex Schramm, 1970

"This (Texas Stadium) is the house that Don Meredith built and that Roger Staubach paid for."
– Broadcaster Frank Gifford on ABC's Monday Night Football

"This was Clint's dream. The stadium has played a major role in the image of class and style the Cowboys have developed in becoming America's Team. Clint's theory was football was an outdoor sport, but fans shouldn't have to sit in the rain."
– Tex Schramm on former team owner Clint Murchison and
the building of Texas Stadium

"Texas Stadium has a hole in its roof so God can watch his favorite team play."
– Former Cowboys linebacker D.D. Lewis

"I was sorry to leave the Cotton Bowl. I liked the crowd better there. They were rowdy. I liked all the beer drinkers, the loud people . . . At Texas Stadium, it was more like a country club . . . Football was becoming more corporate. People started wearing minks to the game. They'd get fully dressed. No more jeans and t-shirts."
– Former Dallas Cowboys defensive back Cornell Green

"Listen, a guy like Calvin Hill comes along every ten years. A guy like Duane Thomas comes along every twenty years."
– Dallas offensive lineman Ralph Neely

"You're laying on the ground in Texas Stadium and you look up through that hole in the sky . . . You wait for the angels to come and take you away through this hole. I hated that place."
  – Former Washington Redskins quarterback Joe Theismann

"If it's the ultimate, how come they're playing it again next year?"
  – Dallas Cowboys running back Duane Thomas on the Super Bowl, 1972

"Sure I've got one. It's a perfect twenty-twenty."
  – Duane Thomas, when asked about his IQ

"Duane Thomas was a Jekyll and Hyde. You never knew how he was going to act, and everybody around him had to go around the edge. I treated Duane differently. I felt we had a mature team that would understand why I did. It wasn't easy. He made every day a challenge."
  – Tom Landry

"Duane (Thomas) is one of the most gifted runners in football today. The reason for his silence was because he wanted to show America how good a football player he was—and it was because of his silence that he was able to do this."
  – Former NFL running back Jim Brown, speaking for his friend Duane Thomas, 1972

"Duane has been good. But I really believe he hasn't yet reached his potential. I used to think that Gale Sayers and Jim Brown were the greatest running backs I ever saw. But some day Thomas will surpass them both. He never gets hurt and he has tremendous speed and timing. And he also has a brilliant football mind."
  – Roger Staubach, 1972

"We thought he (Duane Thomas) was the closest thing to Jim Brown that we had ever seen. He blocked, he caught the ball. He was awesome. His speed and moves for a guy that big were unbelievable. You can't extrapolate a career, but he was one of the most fantastic talents ever to come into the NFL."
   – Bob Ryan of NFL Films

"When I was a kid, I idolized Duane Thomas when he played for the Cowboys . . . If I could be a running back like anybody I've seen, I'd choose his running style. Jim Brown was great and so is O.J. (Simpson), but Duane Thomas was unbelievable."
   – Earl Campbell

"Evidently."
   – Duane Thomas, when asked by Tom Brookshier: "You have a lot of speed for a big man?" after the 1972 Super Bowl victory

"If I read the Constitution right, it gives me the freedom to do as I please. There's no stipulation that says if you play football you have to talk. I don't get paid for talking. I get paid to play football."
   – Duane Thomas, on his refusal to talk to the media

"Duane ran us right into the Super Bowl that year and it just about destroyed the team. A Super Bowl is supposed to bring everybody together and here we were holding up the Super Bowl trophy and everybody is pissed off."
   – Walt Garrison

"I think it's a successful end to our twelve-year plan."
   – Cowboys owner Clint Murchison after the team's first Super Bowl win in 1972

"We'll be back. This was only a start. They can't say we don't win the big one anymore . . . We're going to be like the Yankees and the Celtics—a dynasty."
  – Tex Schramm after the first Dallas Super Bowl win, 1972

"Terry Bradshaw is so dumb that he couldn't spell cat if you spotted him the c and the a."
  – Dallas Cowboys linebacker Thomas "Hollywood" Henderson
    on the Pittsburgh Steelers quarterback

"A two-quarterback system is fine, but the public just won't identify with it. You divide the whole town if you have two quarterbacks, and there's so much talk about it, it's distracting."
  – Dallas Cowboys coach Tom Landry, 1973

"Tom really admired the way Craig Morton read defenses. He read them a lot better than Roger. Roger had the tendency to look at one receiver and then pull the ball down and run . . . Roger wasn't a true passer. He was a true runner who learned to pass later in his life, and became a great one, but it wasn't his true calling to throw a football. To go back and fake a pass and run, that was his true instinct."
  – Former Dallas Cowboys middle linebacker Lee Roy Jordan

"I don't know what to say. I'm waiting for Coach Landry to send someone in with a statement."
  – Roger Staubach, after accepting a Touchdown Club award,
    referring to Landry's play-calling

"The only guy who ever had an effect on the Cowboys by being put into the game was Roger Staubach. Otherwise, every time Tom ever replaced a starting quarterback with a backup quarterback, he lost."
  – Former Dallas Cowboys receiver Pete Gent

"Losing to Dallas was the worst feeling in the world. You'd rather have your arm cut off."
— Former Washington Redskins defender Diron Talbert, 1997

"Go You Dallas Cowboys, Go!"
(Theme song to The Tom Landry TV Show)

Go! Go! Dallas! Cowboys!
Dallas Cowboys stampede down the field,
See the defense reel and watch 'em fall.
Blockers out in front to clear the way,
Show 'em how to win 'em all.
Loyal Cowboy fans stand up and cheer,
Let the whole world hear our bugles blow.
Stand Up! Stampede!
Go you Dallas Cowboys, Go!
Go!
Go! Go!
Go Go Go—Cowboys!
It's the gold team of the senior pros,
Let the whole world hear our bugles blow.
Stand Up! Stampede!
Go you Dallas Cowboys, Go!

"It caught the imagination of so many people, not only because it was the Cowboys and Indians, but the lure of how we romanticized that part of our history. The western expansion. The Sunbelt city, gleaming, neo-traditional architecture versus the sophisticated East, the center of power."
— Former Dallas Cowboys running back Calvin Hill, on the Cowboys-Redskins rivalry

"Psychology has won very few football games. Football is still blocking and tackling. If it was a game of psychology, psychologists would play the game. Instead of Dick Butkus, you'd have Dr. Joyce Brothers at middle linebacker."
– Former Dallas Cowboys running back Walt Garrison

"Every year it takes the coaches a few games to remember we're human."
– Dallas defensive lineman Bob Lilly, 1971

"Lee Roy Jordan was the team leader and very helpful to me. He was kind of like the perfect Dallas Cowboy, the guy who set the example."
– Former Dallas Cowboys defensive lineman Randy White

"Bob was the best lineman I ever saw. He combined great strength with quickness. It was kind of uncanny the things he did. Two or three men blocking him every play, and he still goes in and traps the passer."
– Tom Landry on Bob Lilly

"He's (Lilly) the only player I ever remember who, when we'd watch our defensive films, other guys would oooh and aaah and talk about what he did."
– Roger Staubach

"Right after White grabbed me by the ankles and dangled my body out the window from the eleventh floor."
– Dallas personnel director Gil Brandt, when asked how and when he came to contract terms with defensive tackle Randy White

"The guard came up to me and said, 'I can't block him.' Just like that, 'I can't block him.' You don't know how frightening that was. I looked at the guy and wanted to say, 'What do you want me to do? Do you want to throw the ball and have me try to block him?'"
— Los Angeles Rams quarterback Pat Haden, on talking to his lineman about Randy White

"We don't like the colleges using the wishbone so much because the quarterbacks don't pass enough, blockers don't get used to enough pass-protecting, and running backs don't get to catch enough passes. But the wishbone does get the backs ready to be pro runners."
— Dallas Cowboys assistant coach Ermal Allen, 1976

"It's not whether you win or lose, but who gets the blame."
— Dallas Cowboys lineman Blaine Nye on coach Tom Landry's critical film review sessions

"If the WFL succeeds, I don't want to sign their players. I want to sign their accountants."
— Clint Murchison on the financially struggling World Football League

"I never really did say the Hail Mary. I was joking in the locker room afterward about closing my eyes and saying the Hail Mary. I would have joked I'd said a prayer, but being Catholic, I reflectively used the term, 'Hail Mary.'"
— Roger Staubach, on his last-minute miracle game-winning pass to Drew Pearson to beat Minnesota in a playoff game

"The Cowboys were in the Super Bowl last season, and I didn't see them graduating any seniors."
– New Philadelphia Eagles coach Dick Vermeil, on why Dallas was the team to beat in 1976

"For an eighty-four-year-old Indian, he showed me some moves."
– Dallas Cowboys defensive back Charlie Waters, after watching a computerized football game involving a mythical team of greats, including Jim Thorpe

"Tackling him is like tackling a shot put."
– Dallas Cowboys linebacker Dave Edwards on teammate Robert Newhouse

"When his career is over, there probably won't be many NFL records that won't have his name on them."
– O.J. Simpson on Tony Dorsett

"He was one of my favorite guys, even though he suffered from Dorsett Disease. What was that? He'd say something and then apologize later . . . Of course he was cocky. He was the best damned running back on the planet for fifteen years, why shouldn't he be cocky?"
– Dallas Cowboys publicist Doug Todd on Tony Dorsett

"We were used to winning and the town was used to seeing us win . . . the whole state, actually. People began to identify with us, because we were the team on television, on Monday night games . . . We got national exposure, and we expected it to benefit us in our own area. We helped make the town more popular, too. I remember one year we went up to Pittsburgh to play the Steelers

in one of those off-season basketball games and we drew over 8,000 people. That was how we became America's team."
    –Former Dallas receiver Drew Pearson

"The Cowboys were conceived as America's Team. We were the clean-cut team. It's because of Roger. They developed his image because that's what he was—Captain America."
    – Former Cowboys defensive back Cliff Harris

"I hated 'America's Team.' It became bulletin-board material for every team in the league. PR people didn't have to go out on the field and face those other guys."
    – Dallas quarterback Danny White

"If they're America's Team, we must be Texas' team."
    – Houston Oilers coach Bum Phillips after beating Dallas

"Even if you've only tried out for the Cowboys, you're a hero."
    – Former Dallas Cowboys defensive lineman Harvey Martin

"When I first came to the Cowboys, I felt like I was becoming part of a legend. I mean, they had always been winners, far back as I can remember. It was kind of special, thinking about the Dallas Cowboys, and them making me their first draft choice."
    – Randy White

"The two most important people to CBS are J.R. Ewing and Tom Landry. Our ratings are up this season, and there's only one reason: The Cowboys."
    – CBS-TV spokesman Beano Cook on the "Dallas" prime-time television show and the Cowboys

"The Cowboys are the most overrated, over-hyped team in professional football."
– ABC-TV sportscaster Howard Cosell

"The Cowboys became a vehicle that projected Dallas as a winner instead of the 'Killer of Kennedy.'"
– Former Cowboys linebacker and assistant coach Jerry Tubbs

Cowboys Head Coaches And Their Records

1960-88: Tom Landry (270-178-6)
1989-93: Jimmy Johnson (51 37)
1994-97: Barry Switzer (45-26)
1998-99: Chan Gailey (18-16)
2000-02: Dave Campo (15-33)
2003-   Bill Parcells (25-24)

"Outside of the Cowboys, he (Buddy Ryan) hates the media more than anything else, but he uses the press to twist things, or to get the other team thinking the way he wants them thinking."
– Cowboys linebacker Garry Cobb, who previously played for Buddy Ryan's Philadelphia Eagles

"He's just telling us, 'they're number one.'"
– ABC Monday Night Football broadcaster Don Meredith, when a fan made an obscene gesture to the camera

"Cowboy fans love you, win or tie."
– Roger Staubach

"Dallas fans never feel the Cowboys have lost a game. It's always that the referees screwed 'em or the Good Lord looked the other way or something."
– CBS-TV broadcaster Tom Brookshier

"Sagebrush, U.S.A. Their fans don't know football, they just know something's wrong if the Cowboys aren't winning by two TD's."
– Tom Brookshier

"We're the second most (hated team). We'll never catch Dallas."
– Raiders managing general partner Al Davis

"Talk to anyone around the league and they'll tell you, 'We don't care who wins, as long as it isn't the Cowboys.'"
– Pittsburgh linebacker Jack Lambert

"The Cowboys are like a woman who's had a lot of facelifts. They're a fantasy from their uniforms to their stadium, which is like being in a living room. They have this holier-than-thou attitude that makes me sick."
– Raiders defensive end Howie Long

"There just aren't enough good-looking girls in Green Bay for the Dallas Cowboys cheerleader look."
– Former Green Bay receiver Max McGee

"I played there (Dallas) when I was with the Bears. I borrowed Roger Stillwell's helmet on the sidelines. Biggest hat on the team, size eight. I took out the cheek pads so it would swivel freely on my head, and I turned it around so the face bar was facing the field. And I turned my head and watched the cheerleaders through the earhole."
– Former Bears halfback Mike Adamle

"Whether you like this kind of shtick or loathe it, you must admit that the sight of a Dallas Cowboy cheerleader shimmying in the Texas moonlight is one of the great by-products of the Industrial Age."
– Journalist Dick Friedman

"When you stare at the Dallas cowgirls you're not staring at talent. You look at most of the moves, the gyration, the twisting, what they wear, it's really a sexual symbolism. Anybody who sees no relation to sex is either blind, deaf and dumb, or all of them."
– Psychology professor Thomas Tutko

"The triumph of an uncluttered mind."
– Dallas offensive lineman Blaine Nye, on backup quarterback Clint Longley's performance in leading the Cowboys to a come-from-behind victory against Washington on Thanksgiving Day, 1974

"I think Roger Staubach is a real-life hero. And I honestly believe the Cheerleaders are real-life heroines to a lot of people in this country. They represent America and all that's good about it. I understand that where little girls used to dream of being Miss America, now they dream of becoming a cheerleader for the Cowboys instead."
– Dallas Cowboys cheerleader director Suzanne Mitchell

"Craig's a good quarterback . . . but Roger can be a great one. I mean, a Unitas. This guy is fantastic, wait and see."
– Dallas assistant coach Ermal Allen on quarterbacks Morton and Staubach

"If Tom were going to create a quarterback, it would be Roger Staubach. Roger is the ideal quarterback for Tom, for the Cowboys, for the system."
    — Former Dallas Cowboys quarterback Don Meredith

**"His idea of breaking training is putting
whipped cream on his pie."**
— Dallas sportswriter Bob St. John on Roger
Staubach's All-American image

"We've got to do something about this guy (Staubach). He's going to ruin the image of an NFL quarterback if he doesn't start smoking, drinking, cussing, or something."
    — Don Meredith

"I probably enjoy sex more than Joe Namath. The difference is I enjoy it with one woman: my wife."
    — Roger Staubach, early 1970s

"Roger Staubach was an incredible talent. He exemplified the spirit of a gladiator football player. Roger Staubach was and is one of my idols . . . Roger was a Dr. Jekyll and Mr. Hyde kind of a guy. This man with impeccable ethics, faithful to his wife, a Christian, but then he was this crazy football player, this guy with the drive to just whip your ass, this competitive thing."
    — Thomas "Hollywood" Henderson

"He (Staubach) was the greatest hero of his time . . . He was the hero of a nation, not just of the Cowboys or even the league."
    — Tex Schramm

"If Roger wants me, I'll be in Dallas next week, and he knows where he can find me. If he wants to go fifteen rounds in Memorial Auditorium, he can even promote it."
– Dallas backup quarterback Clint Longley, on his feud with Staubach

"When you talk about great quarterbacks, Roger has to stand alongside Otto Graham and Johnny Unitas, of all the ones I can recall. Mainly because he was such a consistent performer and one of the great two-minute clutch players—like Bobby Layne in his prime. I don't know of any quarterback I played against or watched who I'd rather have than Roger."
– Tom Landry

"He runs like a sissy."
– Broadcaster Alex Hawkins on Staubach

"He's (Tom Landry) a perfectionist. If he was married to Raquel Welch, he'd expect her to cook."
– Don Meredith

"You can't show emotion. I trained myself from watching Ben Hogan. He never let his concentration break."
– Tom Landry

"I don't believe you can be emotional and concentrate the way you must to be effective. When I see a great play from the sideline, I can't cheer it . . . The players don't want to see me rushing around and screaming. They want to believe I know what I'm doing."
– Tom Landry

"He's (Landry) a plastic man, actually no man at all."
– Duane Thomas, 1971

"He's (Landry) the man in the funny hat."
– Roger Staubach

"He's (Landry) a man of tremendous emotion. He's got great compassion for people that you really get to know about only when you become close to him. He's a very warm person and he's very giving and he sacrifices greatly for the team, more than probably anybody. He works harder than anybody I've ever known in my life."
– Dallas Cowboys quarterback Craig Morton, 1972

"Playing for Coach Landry was not some high school picnic, you know? . . . You could always tell when a game meant more to him, too. He was pretty level, usually, but he always told us how important it would be to win in New York. He'd tell us if we wanted to get known, to make the Pro Bowl teams, to have magazine stories written about us, then we had better win in New York. He said we had to have a good game against the Giants, because that's where all the publicity was, all the television networks, the big newspapers."
– Randy White

"I think he had all the qualifications a perfect coach has to have. He had endless patience . . . he was a great teacher . . . he was perfectly prepared, always knew what to do in any crisis situation."
– Tony Dorsett on Landry

"When I first became a Dallas Cowboy, Landry was this dictator, this Castro, this Khrushchev, this Saddam Hussein, this Ayatollah.

You know. You didn't talk back. It was religious. It was communism. It was all these things you fear, and people marched around like they were in the Red Army . . . It never occurred to me to be afraid of Landry. It never occurred to me to take him as seriously as he thought he was."
– Thomas "Hollywood" Henderson

"As a player, I detested Tom Landry. He was so mechanical and distant. I left the Dallas Cowboys in 1974 after five years, in part to escape his suffocating ethic."
– Former Cowboys lineman Pat Toomay

"He's (Tex Schramm) sick, demented, and dishonest."
– Duane Thomas, 1971

"That's not bad. He got two out of three."
– Tex Schramm responding to Thomas's remarks about him, 1971

"Tom was not a very honest person with players. People don't want to admit that because they want to sit up there and say, 'Well, he was a Christian man' and so forth. I'm quite sure Jack the Ripper was a Christian . . . He (Landry) was one of the most ruthless and coldhearted son of a guns I ever met in my life in terms of a coach and just a human being."
– Duane Thomas on Landry

"When I came Landry motivated us by that fear to perform for him. If you didn't perform, you were out. He prepared us . . . But he

wasn't the motivator. He couldn't give a pre-game pep talk. Lee Roy (Jordan) was that guy. He was that kind of leader. I loved that guy."
   – Drew Pearson

"There was a rumor going around camp that Duane and the Muslims were going to kidnap Tex. Next morning, Tex had four or five guards around him. It was wild."
   – Dallas running back Calvin Hill

"I feel like a rat in a cheese factory with the cat on vacation."
   – Dallas linebacker "Hollywood" Henderson, on being on a
      world championship team, 1978

"I was the best linebacker to ever play in the National Football League. And I didn't play long. But I was the best there was. Before there was an L.T. (Lawrence Taylor), there was a T.H. I made 56 the glamorous number that it is today."
   – "Hollywood" Henderson

"On Thomas's list of priorities, (winning) ranked somewhere below sex and drugs."
   – Harvey Martin, on "Hollywood" Henderson

"The guy (Thomas Henderson) had more ability than anybody who ever played defense for the Cowboys. He could have been the greatest player ever to play for the Cowboys. But he had another agenda. He wanted to be the greatest partyer, the greatest womanizer in Cowboy history, and he won that . . . He was an All-Pro at partying."
   – Drew Pearson

"I'm more famous than the Shah of Iran."
– "Hollywood" Henderson to reporters prior to a Super Bowl
game against the Pittsburgh Steelers

"Hollywood was sort of an alter-ego of drug addiction and
women. Hollywood never played football. He was hanging out with
Marvin Gaye and doing wild things."
– Thomas Henderson

**"I don't know. I only played there
nine years."**
**– Walt Garrison, when asked if Tom Landry
ever smiles**

"Thomas (Henderson) was probably the greatest athlete . . . and
that's a damned strong statement for me to make . . . that I have
ever seen in my days of playing football. Thomas Henderson was
the best, better than Herschel Walker, Tony Dorsett, any of them.
The best, as far as having athletic ability . . . But he was a loud guy,
a jive guy, a colorful guy."
– Randy White

"But in Super Bowl XIII, like Elvis's voice, my legs never failed
me. So that day I played the finest football game of my career . . .
You won't see a better performance of a football player."
– "Hollywood" Henderson

"I'm the most famous ex-cocaine addict in the world."
– "Hollywood" Henderson

"Too Tall had great ability but limited desire. If he had been motivated to be the best of all time, he could have become consistent and become the best."
— Tom Landry on defensive end Ed "Too Tall" Jones

"It took fourteen years, but Craig Morton finally won a Super Bowl for the Dallas Cowboys."
— First paragraph in a game story written by David Israel of the Chicago Tribune, after Denver quarterback Morton's mistakes helped Dallas win Super Bowl XII

"If its and buts were candy and nuts, we'd all have a Merry Christmas."
— Don Meredith

"Turn out the lights . . . "
— Don Meredith, singing when a game was out of reach on NFL Monday Night Football

THIRD QUARTER
Socks and Jocks (1980s)

As Tom Landry and the Cowboys began their third decade of NFL play, adjustments had to be made.

Prior to the start of the 1980 season, quarterback Roger Staubach announced his retirement. Capable backup Danny White would take the reins and guide the team to five playoff appearances in nine years. Although Dallas made it to the NFC Championship Game on three occasions during that time period, it could never advance to the Super Bowl.

The team's fortunes really began to decline in 1986, as the Cowboys posted a 7-9 record—snapping their streak of twenty consecutive winning seasons. Two years earlier, a group headed by Dallas businessman H.R. "Bum" Bright purchased the team from Clint Murchison.

The now legendary Landry, facing mounting criticism from fans and the media, watched as his '87 and '88 teams fared no better than 7-8 and 3-13. Failed drafts and an aging team with aging systems were catching up with an aging Landry. Even the addition of superstar running back Herschel Walker failed to stem the tide.

Then, on February 25, 1989, Arkansas businessman Jerry Jones purchased the team. In a swift and shocking move, he immediately dumped the "only coach the Cowboys have ever had" in favor of

University of Miami coach Jimmy Johnson. Soon joining Landry in the exit line were President/General Manager Tex Schramm and Player Personnel Director Gil Brandt.

New owner Jones, basking in the limelight, irritated fans by proudly announcing: "My entire office and business will be at this (Valley Ranch training) complex. I intend to have an understanding of the complete situation, an understanding of the player situation, of the socks and jocks."

Shortly thereafter, a flurry of player personnel moves took place; quarterback Danny White retired; the Cowboys traded running back Herschel Walker to the Minnesota Vikings for five veteran players and eight draft choices; and, with the first pick in the NFL draft, the team selected UCLA quarterback Troy Aikman.

Under first-year coach Johnson, Dallas hit rock bottom in 1989, posting a 1-15 record.

* * *

"Anybody can have an off decade."
– Cowboys defensive lineman Larry Cole, who scored three touchdowns in 1968-69 on fumbles and interceptions, and another one in 1980

"If England was so nice, why did everybody leave and come to America?"
– Dallas Cowboys tight end Doug Cosbie

"I think John is a young Tom Landry . . . John is very bright, and he would be a great senator, a great banker. If he has one fault it's that he's not a motivator of people, just like Tom (Landry). He understands that he has a great plan, he's got talented players, and

he thinks he shouldn't have to slap somebody on the back to get them to play hard."
 – Former Cowboys personnel director Gil Brandt, on former Dallas assistant coach John Mackovic

"That little monkey gets loose, doesn't he?"
 – Broadcaster Howard Cosell on the elusiveness of Washington Redskins running back Alvin Garrett during an ABC Monday Night football game against Dallas, 1983

Memorable Nicknames

"Dandy Don" Meredith
Thomas "Hollywood" Henderson
"Bullet Bob" Hayes
"The Manster" (Randy White)
Ed "Too Tall" Jones
"Captain America" (Roger Staubach)
"The Triplets" (Troy Aikman, Emmitt Smith, Michael Irvin)
Daryl "Moose" Johnston
"Captain Crash" (Cliff Harris)

"I injured everything. I injured my transverse processes once. Most people don't even know what your transverse processes are— those little spurs that come out of the base of your spine."
 – Former Dallas Cowboys linebacker D.D. Lewis

"I didn't know the rule, and I didn't have time to look it up."
 – Dallas Cowboys kick returner Steve Wilson after fumbling a kick into the end zone and not realizing that he could have downed it

"Holding, number 75, offense."
– Frequent public address announcement by NFL referees on
Dallas offensive lineman Phil Pozderac during the mid-1980s

"I have never felt like this. I have never felt like kissing a 270-
pound man."
– Dallas Cowboys quarterback Danny White on hugging
defensive end Jim Jeffcoat, who returned an interception
sixty-five yards for a score in a win over the Giants, 1985

"No, no, Danny, no!"
– Dallas Cowboys coach Tom Landry shouting from the sideline
to Danny White, who faked a punt against Washington, 1983

**"He (Franco Harris) faked me out so bad one
time that I got a fifteen-yard penalty for
grabbing my own facemask."**
**– D.D. Lewis, on the elusive Pittsburgh
Steelers running back**

"His numbers are slightly higher than Staubach's. But I can close
my eyes and see Staubach putting the ball on the money twenty
yards downfield, and when I think of White I see an eight-yard com-
pletion on third-and-ten."
– Sportswriter Paul Zimmerman, 1984

"I've decided to go with Pozderac at quarterback, uh, I mean
Hogeboom."
– Tom Landry, announcing his decision to start Gary Hogeboom
over Danny White

"The guy's got a year's supply of dried food in his basement. He's got phone numbers to call when Armageddon arrives. That's the kind of guy you want quarterbacking your team, down seventeen points with the time running down?"
    – Former Dallas receiver Pete Gent on Danny White, 1983

"I don't remember very many specifics. I can't remember games that I played. I can't remember even playing at Texas Stadium. I can't remember anything clearly. It's kind of a strange thing, but I know I did it. I know I was there. I know it wasn't a dream. I don't know if it was the concussions or what."
    – Danny White trying to recall his career with the Cowboys

"Danny was probably the most underrated player Dallas ever had. He was a great quarterback, with skills I never had, with skills Morton and Meredith never had. But for some reason I still don't understand, the team seemed to turn on him. When Tom honored that, and gave the job to Hogeboom instead of Danny, it was a critical error. The team never recovered from it, either. Nor did Danny ever get over it . . . believe me, he could have been the best Cowboy quarterback ever."
    – Former Dallas Cowboys quarterback Roger Staubach

"It's really impossible to judge quarterbacks because it's the most dependent position on the team. So much depends on the people around you. We were definitely a team in transition, and I will always be judged accordingly. But I felt good about what I did as quarterback."
    – Danny White

"To be successful in professional sports, you have to be involved in activities that put pressure on a marriage and family life. The football player in me, and the competitive person that I am, would

have loved to have gone to and won a Super Bowl, two or three. Maybe it's better that I didn't go to or win a Super Bowl."
– Danny White

"When I came to the Cowboys, they didn't even have any extra-large shorts. The biggest size they had was large. I got the first extra-large ones."
– Dallas offensive tackle Nate Newton, 1988

"There was a time when I expected too much from people. I was looking for perfection. I could never accept a player who didn't do his best. I wasn't very tolerant of players who weren't willing to put out. But you have to blend all types of players to make a successful team."
– Tom Landry

"Any man that can be as destructive on the field as Arnold Schwarzenegger is in the movies, yet as compassionate and down-to-earth off the field as Mother Teresa, that's a heck of a man."
– Former Cowboys assistant coach Ernie Stautner on
  Randy White

"Tom Landry told me it's not that hard to become a great football coach. He said it's all in how you wear the hat."
– Actor Gary Busey, on preparing to play Bear Bryant in a
  movie, 1983

"To me, the ideal coach would be a combination of Tom Landry and Bum Phillips."
– Former NFL receiver Mike Renfro

"We didn't coach him, we just aimed him."
– Gary Phillips, Herschel Walker's high school coach in Georgia

"I hate to think what he might do once he's comfortable in Tom's system and the coaching staff has had time to really figure out how to use him. I think there's a good chance Herschel Walker will cause the same kind of defensive re-thinking in the league that Bob Hayes did when he brought his Olympic speed to the Cowboys."
  – St. Louis Cardinals head coach and former Cowboys assistant Gene Stallings on Walker's potential

---

Starting Quarterbacks For Season Openers

1960-62: Eddie LeBaron
1963-68: Don Meredith
1969-70: Roger Staubach
1971-72: Craig Morton
1973-79: Roger Staubach
1980-83: Danny White
1984: Gary Hogeboom
1985-87: Danny White
1988: Steve Pelluer
1989-99: Troy Aikman
2000: Randall Cunningham
2001-03: Quincy Carter
2004: Vinny Testaverde
2005: Drew Bledsoe

"I've never believed that any one player can make or break a team. This is a team sport and we have a lot of people on the Cowboys who are going to play a major role in getting us back to where we feel we belong. I'm just looking forward to getting the chance to do whatever I can."
  – Dallas Cowboys running back Herschel Walker

"I get horrified sometimes at our play calling. I've heard we're not using certain players because they haven't been brought along yet. Maybe the problem is we can't utilize the talent of certain guys because we don't have anybody to direct how to use them. It doesn't seem we have anybody in charge that knows what they're doing."
— Dallas Cowboys owner Bum Bright, during a tough 1987 season

"He knew more about football and probably still knows more about the all-around game than anyone now . . . I felt like I knew him, and I respect him as one of the great human beings I've ever been around."
— Former Cowboys defensive back Bill Bates on Tom Landry

"From all these people who want to fire Landry, I want to know one thing: Who's going to replace him? It's like replacing Vince Lombardi. I guarantee you that ten years from now everybody will be saying, 'Yeah, but this guy is no Tom Landry.'"
— Dallas Cowboys defensive back Everson Walls, 1988

"I remember, even at the height of his success, he'd look around on the sideline and yell for a player who had been gone for three years."
— Dallas Cowboys general manager Tex Schramm on coach
  Tom Landry, 1988

"After that year (1985), Tom told me he was thinking about when he was going to retire and I had better start making some changes, so we could have a clean transition. That's when I started going out and looking for the best young coaches with a lot of potential . . . I had some good ones lined up. I got Wade Phillips to be the defensive coordinator. I had Marty Schottenheimer lined up to take Tom's place, after he got fired in Cleveland, but before

he got hired in Kansas City. I took Schottenheimer around looking at houses . . . (Then) Tom gave up the idea of retiring."
  – Tex Schramm

"It's the end of an era, our era. A lot of old Cowboys are crying tonight."
  – Former Dallas Cowboys defensive lineman Bob Lilly on the firing of Tom Landry, 1989

"He (Landry) is like a John the Baptist to me . . . In football, I consider him the greatest coach in American history."
  – Rev. Billy Graham

"To me, Tom Landry is the greatest coach in the history of the game."
– Roger Staubach

"Landry was a great football coach. You can pick on his weaknesses, but you have to look at history. Over a long period, what he did was pretty darn good."
  – Roger Staubach

"I don't think Coach Landry should be judged on the number of games he won. He should be judged on the number of lives he influenced. He had a higher winning percentage doing that than winning games."
  – Former Cowboys defensive back Charlie Waters

"Obviously, Tom Landry was a great coach and a real solid man. He was someone everyone respected—his players, your players,

other coaches, officials, fans. Landry was so innovative. You think of him as a defensive coach, but his biggest innovation was in offense, with all the movement and shifting. Every team does that today, but Tom Landry was the one who started it."
    – CBS-TV football analyst John Madden

"In the workforce, you look for people with great character, and Landry was the same way. If you look at what kind of people we had, character was the Cowboys."
    – Former Cowboys quarterback Danny White

"He coached the Cowboys for twenty-nine years, and almost none of the losses can be blamed on him. I don't think a decision of his, pure and simple, ever cost the Cowboys a game. I really don't. And that's amazing, that is really amazing. I credit most of it, most of the success and the winning, to his preparation. Nobody was better prepared for a game than Tom Landry."
    – Roger Staubach

"Tom Landry is the single-most important figure in Cowboys' history."
    – New Dallas Cowboys owner Jerry Jones, 1989

"Before I bought the Cowboys, who would succeed Coach Landry was not foremost in my mind . . . I had a list. I went back to my past. Jimmy Johnson was on it. I also reflected on Barry Switzer. There was a third name, but before I contacted him, I decided he would not be interested in returning to coaching. That was Frank Broyles, the former coach at Arkansas who is now the school's athletic director. He would have been an outstanding coach for the Cowboys."
    – Jerry Jones

"I don't expect to replace Tom Landry. All I can ask is just let me do my thing, let me work, let me show my enthusiasm and judge me by what happens later."
– Newly hired head-coach Jimmy Johnson, 1989

"I think Tom Landry is one of the finest individuals and finest coaches that I would ever hope to know. And it hurts me when someone said I did something out of disrespect to Tom Landry. If I did, I'm sorry."
– Jimmy Johnson

"I bought the Cowboys not for financial gain but basically because I'm a frustrated coach."
– Jerry Jones

"Remember, Jimmy has a degree in psychology. We're talking about a genius. He's going to be able to horse-trade with people in the league. There's no question about that."
– Jerry Jones

"History will show that one of the finest things that ever happened to the Dallas Cowboys is Jimmy Johnson."
– Jerry Jones, 1989

"Jimmy Johnson will be worth five Heisman Trophy winners and five first-round draft choices."
– Jerry Jones, 1989

"When Jerry and I talked, we agreed that we were going to Dallas together for our last stop. From the first day I came here, I viewed this as my last job."
– Jimmy Johnson, 1989

"My entire office and business will be at this (Valley Ranch) complex. I intend to have an understanding of the complete situation, an understanding of the player situation, of the socks and jocks."
– Jerry Jones

"Whatever Mr. Jones did, he was within his rights. He owns the team, and I imagine if a man spends that much money on a football team, he has the right to decide who should coach it."
– Tom Landry

"They're taking Aikman to sell tickets . . . The Cowboys have done everything in their power to embarrass the greatest NFL franchise in the past thirty years."
– ESPN draft analyst Joe Theismann, criticizing the Cowboys for picking Troy Aikman number one in the 1989 draft over Michigan State offensive lineman Tony Mandarich

"Winning and losing concerns me, but what concerns me more is when you take away from the integrity of the game. It was confirmed last night that there was a $200 bounty on Luis Zendejas and a $500 bounty on Troy Aikman. An Eagles coach and two Eagles players confirmed it. That's not the way the game is supposed to be played. I will be filing a complaint . . . But our day will come."
– Jimmy Johnson, after a 27-0 loss to the Eagles in the infamous Bounty Bowl in 1989

"I would have said something to him, but he wouldn't stay on the field long enough. He got his fat rear end in the dressing room."
— Jimmy Johnson, on confronting Buddy Ryan after the Bounty Bowl

"That's ridiculous. I don't send anybody after anybody. Players talk about that crap all the time. I don't put bounties on anybody."
— Buddy Ryan, responding to Johnson's bounty charge

"I can sit here today and honestly say I don't think there has ever been anybody in this league to win only one game and be as excited about the future as I am. Even though we're sitting here at 1-15, I don't believe there are too many people in this league that don't believe the Dallas Cowboys can be a championship football team again."
— Jerry Jones, after the 1989 season

FOURTH QUARTER
Jimmy, Jerry, Barry, and Chan (1990s)

"The Good, the Bad, and the Ugly" might best describe the Dallas Cowboys in the 1990s.

The Good: Coach Jimmy Johnson quickly rebuilt the team, leading Dallas back to the playoffs in 1991. Led by quarterback Troy Aikman, the number one draft pick in 1989, and running back Emmitt Smith, Johnson's Cowboys won back-to-back Super Bowls, beating Buffalo both times, on January 31, 1993, and January 30, 1994. Two years later, the Cowboys, now under coach Barry Switzer, added another Super Bowl trophy to their collection.

The Bad: The power struggle between owner Jerry Jones and the no-nonsense Johnson reared its ugly head in March of 1994. Johnson abruptly resigned, and Jones brought in Switzer, the former University of Oklahoma coach with no NFL experience. In fact, Switzer had been out of coaching entirely for five years before he accepted the call from Jones.

Although constantly criticized by fans and the media for his less-than-hands-on approach to coaching, Switzer directed the Cowboys to a division title in 1994 and a Super Bowl crown on January 28, 1996.

After losing in the divisional championship game in 1996, things went downhill quickly for Switzer and company. The team plummeted to a 6-10 record in 1997, and Switzer was forced to resign. After a month-long search, Jones hired little-known Pittsburgh Steelers offensive coordinator Chan Gailey as the Cowboys' fourth head coach.

The Ugly: Switzer's tenure was marked by a series of embarrassing off-the-field incidents, reminiscent of his days of loose discipline at OU. Defensive lineman Leon Lett was suspended by the NFL for failing a drug test. Offensive lineman Erick Williams was nearly killed in an alcohol-related automobile accident. Wide receiver Michael Irvin drew a suspension from the league after a much-publicized drug and sex scandal.

The star on the helmet of "America's Team" had suddenly lost its shine. Instead, the Cowboys were ridiculed by the media and on late-night TV. Jones vowed to clean up the tarnished image and hired former player Calvin Hill as a counselor. Then, in the summer of 1997, prior to his last season as Dallas' coach, Switzer was arrested for carrying a concealed handgun at the Dallas Fort-Worth Regional Airport.

Gailey led the team to a 10-6 mark in 1998, but after a 8-8 season the following year, he was fired.

And in 1999, former coach Tom Landry died of leukemia.

* * *

"He (Troy Aikman) isn't just one of those rawboned quarterbacks who looks good in the shower."

– Jerry Jones

"They're the pick of the litter."

– Jerry Jones, on the Cowboys cheerleaders

"Next to Coach (Bear) Bryant, Jimmy Johnson is the best I've ever been around."
– Dallas Cowboys scouting director Larry Lacewell, 1993

"In all of my years of coaching, I've never ever, ever seen a game officiated as poorly as this one. Call after call after call after call, including replays. Unbelievable . . . and not just judgment calls. There's no way in this world I can go without saying something about four or five of the worst calls I've ever seen in my life. If that had been a coaching staff out there, they would have been fired."
– Jimmy Johnson after a 22-9 loss to the New York Giants in 1991

"When we started to win some games, Coach Johnson got on a high you wouldn't believe. I think he was like a manic-depressive. A lot of coaches tell you winning is the only thing, but when it came to winning, well, Coach Johnson was just crazy about it."
– Nate Newton

"The only time Jimmy Johnson didn't run up the score was twenty-seven years ago when he took the SAT."
– CBS-TV sportscaster Jim Nantz

"Of course, the one thing I would not want to see is for Jimmy to wind up in a mental institution."
– Jerry Jones

"I've had a touch of burnout every year for twenty-nine seasons of coaching. But give me about a week in the Bahamas, and I'm ready to go again."
– Jimmy Johnson

"I'm not concerned about whether people think I'm a good coach. All I do is win."
– Jimmy Johnson

"We will win the ballgame. And you can put it in three-inch headlines. We will win the ballgame."
– Jimmy Johnson, predicting victory over San Francisco in the 1994 NFC title game

"The man's got balls, I'll say that. I don't know if they're brass or papier-mache. We'll find out pretty soon."
– San Francisco coach George Seifert, responding to Johnson's prediction, 1994

"I'm not much of a historian. I just know that we've won two Super Bowls in a row."
– Jimmy Johnson after Super Bowl XXVIII, 1994

"I think these boys are a miraculous team. They really are . . . It's part of what's added to a new Texas pride."
– Texas Gov. Ann Richards, 1994

"The Cowboys have done a good job bringing back the team. With all of those draft choices, it is hard to miss, but you have to give them credit for making the Herschel Walker deal. If I had stayed, I don't think I would have traded Herschel."
– Tom Landry

"Dallas has the best quarterback in the country, the best quarterback in the universe. They might be playing football on Mars or Pluto, but if they are, Troy Aikman would be better than anybody they have there, too."
– Former Oklahoma coach Barry Switzer, 1994

"Troy Aikman is the best quarterback in the NFL. He's going to the Hall of Fame. There's nothing he can't do physically, and he's mentally tough, too. He plays just as hard now after winning it all. He's mentally driven to be the best. And he is the best."
– Roger Staubach

"How 'bout them Cowboys!"
– Dallas coach Jimmy Johnson after beating
San Francisco for the NFC championship, 1993

"I think it would be foolish for me to say I am not going to go into the Ring of Honor because I am mad at Jerry or somebody else. That is foolishness, because I am not at all. It was never a problem with any feelings I had towards the new management and the football team. The thing that hurts me the most is when people say that I'm unforgiving with Jerry and all. That never entered my mind from the time I got out of football because I was really looking to get out of football at the time. The move didn't bother me, really, too much. I guess Jerry and I would agree that maybe we could have done it a little differently."
– Tom Landry, on finally accepting Jerry Jones' invitation to be added to the Cowboys' Ring of Honor in 1993

"The (Philadelphia) Eagles without (quarterback Randall) Cunningham is like Gotham City without Batman."
– Cowboys linebacker Jack Del Rio

"It would be nice to have a dome in Dallas. Growing up in Cooper (Texas), you wonder why they never closed the roof."
– Pittsburgh Steelers running back Byron "Bam" Morris, 1996

"The Cowboys are America's Team. Dallas has the babes, the glitz, the uniforms. The Cowboys are the American dream. Houston (Oilers) is Texas's team. It's a cowtown compared to Dallas. Let's face it, what was in Texas before the Cowboys? The Alamo."
– Washington Post columnist Tony Kornheiser, 1994

"The Cowboys were practically Mexico's Team before they were America's Team."
– Pete Abitante, NFL director of international public relations

"My girlfriend knows more football than Jerry."
– Jimmy Johnson

"People are unhappy with how Jimmy behaves when things go wrong. They are upset there is no place in his life for family and Christmas. Do I believe Jimmy is headed for a breakdown? No. He is totally absorbed in football and grew more tense and edgy as the season wore on. But he is highly intelligent and deals with problems quickly when he recognizes them."
– Jerry Jones, January 5, 1993

"I have no intention of making a coaching change. To have this as an issue is a joke."
– Jerry Jones, on rumors of a rift between him and Johnson

"The likelihood of Jimmy coaching somewhere else is extremely remote. Coaching the Dallas Cowboys is the best job in the country, and I'm not concerned about not having a coach."
  – Jerry Jones

"I should have fired him and brought in Barry Switzer. There are 500 coaches who could have won the Super Bowl with our team."
  – Jerry Jones, talking to friends at a bar at the NFL winter
    meetings in Orlando, Florida, 1994

"I'm deeply hurt that after five years of total commitment to the rebuilding of the Cowboys and after two consecutive Super Bowl championships, I have been treated this way."
  – Jimmy Johnson, after hearing owner Jerry Jones say that any-
    one could have coached the team to success, 1994

"We've had hours of candid discussions the last two days and I can sincerely tell you that I feel better today about Jerry Jones as a friend than I have in our entire relationship. After our discussions, we mutually decided I would no longer be the head coach of the Dallas Cowboys."
  – Jimmy Johnson, 1994

"There's no way in the world we could have accomplished what we did without each other. Some people might describe it as rocky, but something about our relationship worked."
  – Jimmy Johnson on Jerry Jones, 1994

"To be coach of the Dallas Cowboys, one of the main criteria is that we can work together."
  – Jerry Jones, on hiring Barry Switzer, 1994

"We've got a job to do and we're going to do it, baby!"
– Newly-hired Dallas coach Barry Switzer, 1994

"I was fortunate to be lying on the couch last week when I had a phone call. I answered the phone, and it was Jerry Jones. Jerry says, 'Two questions. Do you still want to coach, and would you like possibly to think about coaching the Dallas Cowboys?' "
– Barry Switzer

The Cowboys Have Won Five Super Bowls, Lost Three

January 17, 1971: Super Bowl V
(lost 16-13 to Baltimore)
January 16, 1972: Super Bowl VI
(won 24-3 over Miami)
January 18, 1976: Super Bowl X
(lost 21-17 to Pittsburgh)
January 15, 1978: Super Bowl XII
(won 27-10 over Denver)
January 21, 1979: Super Bowl XIII
(lost 35-31 to Pittsburgh)
January 31, 1993: Super Bowl XXVII
(won 52-17 over Buffalo)
January 30, 1994: Super Bowl XXVIII
(won 30-13 over Buffalo)
January 28, 1996: Super Bowl XXX
(won 27-17 over Pittsburgh)

"It took me five years to put the team together. We'll see what happens with Barry Switzer."
– Jimmy Johnson, 1994

"I think replacing Landry would have been easier. The Cowboys were at the trough, they were down . . . My job is tougher because I've got to follow (Jimmy Johnson's) success."
  – First-year Dallas coach Barry Switzer, 1994

"I read where Barry thinks I'm going to be sitting there taking shots at him. Sounds to me like people in Dallas might be a little paranoid. But if shots are called for, I'll pass them out."
  – Former Cowboys coach Jimmy Johnson on his job as an NFL-TV studio game analyst, 1994

"We all do things differently as coaches. Tom Landry coached them from his tower. Jimmy Johnson coached from a distance. I want to be in there close to where I can feel the heartbeat and pulse of the football team."
  – Barry Switzer, 1994

"Jimmy didn't coach X's and O's in front of players. He let coaches do the coaching. He did the motivating. That's the same way Barry is, except he motivates individually . . . Coach Landry let older players motivate young ones. He wasn't the great motivator."
  – Dallas Cowboys safety Bill Bates, 1997

"These guys know who the boss is. They know they work for me. I make the call on the coaches. Jerry (Jones) and I discussed that. They know that. They know how I work, how the system works. Just because I have a smile on my face, and I'm more fun to work with and be around doesn't mean I can't fire or hire anybody. I've done that before. I've only done it when necessary."
  – Barry Switzer, 1994

"I think he's an outstanding football coach. Of the head coaches I've had, he is, without question, the best motivator I've been around. I think that's the charisma he possesses, the honesty he reveals to his players and the fact he does a great job of communicating at a player's level."
   – Troy Aikman, who played briefly under Switzer at Oklahoma, on Switzer's hiring at Dallas, 1994

"Jerry is a great boss to work for. It's like one of those assistant coaches said the other night: When Jimmy Johnson gets another job out there, he's going to find out there's a hell of a lot worse owners to work for in this league than Jerry Jones."
   – Barry Switzer, 1994

"I kind of believe in fairy tales and Walt Disney, Tinker Bell, Captain Hook and all that. I think we can have a hero come out of this."
   – Barry Switzer on starting unproven Jason Garrett at quarterback, 1994

"I watched Rudy in the morning, Field of Dreams last night, and Jason in between."
   – Barry Switzer on Garrett's remarkable performance against Green Bay, 1994

"You can stick Iowa State up your ass."
   – Cincinnati Bengals coach David Shula, at midfield to Barry Switzer after a 23-20 Dallas victory. Earlier in the week, Switzer had compared the winless Bengals to Iowa State.

"I'm secure. I'm a damn good football coach. I have been all my life."
   – Barry Switzer, 1995

"I think there are a lot of coaches who could have gotten this team where it is. Five-hundred? Hell, no."
 – Jerry Jones, 1995

"I don't give a damn whether I'm considered a great pro coach. That is not important. Nobody wins because of one person. It is the team, the team concepts."
 – Barry Switzer, 1995

"Our goal is to score twenty-seven points a game. If we get two touchdowns and three field goals, we've got our twenty-seven."
 – Barry Switzer

"I wanted to make a foot to control the ball, because if we kick into the wind, they're going to come back and kick a field goal to win the ballgame anyway."
 – Dallas Cowboys coach Barry Switzer on his ill-fated decision to go for it on fourth and one in a 20-17 loss against the Eagles, 1995

"That's a bad call. You can't do that."
 – Fox-TV analyst John Madden on Switzer's fourth down call, 1995

"I think he'd (Switzer) make a great high school coach—but not in Texas."
 – Dallas movie distributor employee Joe DeLaurier, 1995

"That was a grade-school play! You don't go for that in Pop Warner (football)."
 – Garland computer programmer Steve Hamilton, 1995

"There may have been worse decisions made in the annals of time. The Edsel. The leisure suit. Adam biting on the apple."
– Fort Worth Star Telegram columnist Gil LeBreton, 1995

Cowboys Led the Pack in Scouting

The Cowboys were the first team to utilize computer technology while compiling scouting reports in preparation for the NFL draft. Under innovative player personnel director Gil Brandt, Dallas also signed such unknown free agents as Pete Gent and Cornell Green in the early 1960s. Both were basketball players in college, Gent at Michigan State and Green at Utah State. Gent, a receiver, and Green, a defensive back, both contributed to the Cowboys, playing a number of seasons. Some other athletes the team drafted but who went on to fame in other sports:

– Halfback Merv Rettenmund of Ball State was drafted by Dallas in the nineteenth round of the 1965 draft. Rettenmund played baseball for many years with the Baltimore Orioles.

– In 1966, the Cowboys selected Lou Hudson of Minnesota in the twentieth round. Hudson went on to star in the National Basketball Association.

– Dallas picked Pat Riley of Kentucky in the eleventh round of the 1967 draft. Riley played and coached in the NBA.

– And in 1984, Dallas drafted University of Houston track star Carl Lewis in the twelfth round. He stuck with track.

"They went out, bought a team that could beat the Dallas Cowboys and they beat the Dallas Cowboys."
– Cowboys safety James Washington on San Francisco, 1995

"I'm an emotional guy, and I talked about how, in the tough times, you have to be tough. I told them the reason I can handle all of this is because of these personal experiences. You have to be a thick, tough SOB to be in this profession."
– Barry Switzer on talking to his team after the controversial fourth and one play failed against the Eagles, 1995

"You can talk about Deion, his mama, his daddy, his wife and his kids, but don't say a thing about the defense."
– Deion Sanders, after the 20-17 loss to Philadelphia, 1995

"Around here, when you win, it ain't good enough. When you lose, it sure ain't good enough. What is good enough? You guys need to tell us. When you win by thirty? When you win by fifteen?"
– Deion Sanders on the high expectations in Dallas, 1995

**"We did it our way, baby. We did it!
We did it!"**
**– Barry Switzer to Jerry Jones after winning
Super Bowl XXX, 1996**

"They could play this game in Corsicana, in the rain or in the snow and it wouldn't matter. Emotions will be riding high. It's going to be a great collision."
– Cowboys cornerback Kevin Smith on the Dallas-San Francisco NFL championship game, 1995

"Football is a game played by angry men. You have to excite yourself or you won't match the other guy's intensity. This year,

we're throwing caution to the wind. They're not going to try to put you in the hospital, they're going to try to put you in the morgue."
  – Cowboys tight end Scott Galbraith on the upcoming title game with San Francisco, 1995

"When you're down 21-0 and turn the ball over as we did, it puts you in a deep hole. It's like spotting Carl Lewis twenty yards in the 100-yard dash."
  – Dallas Cowboys running back Emmitt Smith after the 38-28 NFL title game loss to San Francisco, 1995

"You're trying to make Barry (Switzer) take the fall. But the last coach I've seen on the damn field was Woody Hayes. That was the last coach I've seen jump on the field and do something, so how are you going to blame Barry Switzer when you don't make a fourth-and-one?"
  – Deion Sanders, 1995

"That's a disgrace to play a championship game on a field like that. Why didn't the league do something about that?"
  – Barry Switzer on the wet turf at Candlestick Park, 1995

"Winning is a great deodorant, and it's all been erased today."
  – Fox-TV analyst John Madden, after Dallas beat Green Bay in the NFL championship game in January 1996, describing the Cowboys' up and down 1995 season

"It's a perfect reflection of the attitude of that organization. They're so arrogant, so prone to insisting that things go their way. They just don't have any idea what it is to be gracious—whether it's in victory or defeat."
  – 49ers president Carmen Policy on the Cowboys' complaints about the Candlestick turf, 1995

"They don't have enough scouts, they don't pay their scouts, and the assistants are underpaid and overworked. Believe me, it's all going to catch up with the Cowboys."
   – Former Cowboys coach Jimmy Johnson, 1995

"Bulletin. What Jerry Jones and Barry Switzer say is going on isn't always what is going on."
   – Dallas Cowboys radio announcer Brad Sham, 1995

"Well, there's good news and bad news. The good news is we won the game. The bad news is I'm going to be back next year—and for some, that is bad news."
   – Barry Switzer, after winning Super Bowl XXX, 1996

   "The fat lady has sung. She's on the way in the limo back to the hotel with us."
   – Dallas Cowboys defensive back Deion Sanders after the
      Cowboys' 27-17 win over Pittsburgh in Super Bowl XXX, 1996

"Everybody I know wanted them (Dallas Cowboys) to lose (in Super Bowl XXX). You wanted them to lose like you wanted Ross Perot to get audited. They're so corporate. Everybody always looks mad, I just think they need to be more fun. They're like the Delta Force of football. They just go in, look real sour, do the job and leave."
   – Dallas author/marketing consultant George Toomer, 1996

"You have a few good friends you can count on. The rest of the people who criticize you or don't like (you) they're all molecules in the spectrum of the universe. I don't care that much what people think anymore."
   – Barry Switzer, 1996

"I know they're ignorant. My critics are people that haven't spent thirty-five years doing what my coaches have done. It's like having a bus driver be a critic for an English or history professor."
– Barry Switzer, 1996

"I don't know what it is he does as head coach."
– Troy Aikman on Barry Switzer

"Don Meredith took the punishment to build the Cowboys' teams that I played on, and Troy (Aikman) took the punishment to build this team. The guy never pointed fingers. He never complained. He took the shots in those early years and he kept coming back."
– Former Dallas quarterback Roger Staubach, 1996

> **"I've always had the ability to put the ball where I wanted it to go, whether it was football or baseball. Now golf, that's another thing."**
> – Troy Aikman, 1996

"I'm not gonna drink RC Cola and double-date with him (Troy Aikman)."
– Barry Switzer on his strained relationship with the Dallas quarterback, 1996

"The only one who can cover me one-on-one is my jersey."
– Michael Irvin

"Jerry Jones dishonors the agreement he made when he came into the NFL partnership. He takes what does not belong to him. The NFL is what we sell. It belongs to thirty teams, not the Dallas Cowboys."
— NFL commissioner Paul Tagliabue on Jones doing his own marketing of sponsors, 1996

"He's (Lamar Hunt) revered. He brought this city a champion. He's really seen as a fan, and that's what he is. In thirty years, I've never seen a sign of an ego from Lamar. I couldn't imagine Lamar having a television show like Jerry Jones."
— Former Kansas City Chiefs quarterback Len Dawson on Chiefs' owner Lamar Hunt, 1995

"In my mind, he's the Michael Jordan of football. A superstar at what he does."
— Cowboys defensive coordinator Dave Campo on Deion Sanders, 1997

"I think he just got his cape out of the cleaners. He's packing it for Pittsburgh."
— Barry Switzer on hobbled baseball-football player Deion Sanders and the upcoming season opener at Pittsburgh, 1997

"We don't carry an 'S' on our chest. We just wear a star on our helmet and try to do the best job we can."
— Cowboys running back Emmitt Smith, 1997

"Sanders couldn't tackle my wife Emma."
— 71-year-old former NFL two-way player Chuck Bednarik on the tackling ability of Deion Sanders, a modern two-way player, 1996

"What's he going to do, arm-tackle me? . . . He's basically just a glorified flag-football player who can run."
– Philadelphia Phillies pitcher Curt Schilling on throwing inside at Deion Sanders during the on-going feud, 1997

"I didn't think the defensive coaches this year did a good job at all . . . They need to go out and get a qualified guy to come in and teach these young guys . . . but as usual, they'll probably go in-house and get an unqualified guy in there."
– Dallas Cowboys defensive lineman Charles Haley, 1996

"Terry Bradshaw is obviously smarter than I am. He made much smarter life decisions than I did."
– Former Dallas Cowboys linebacker Thomas "Hollywood" Henderson, whose career was ended by drugs and alcohol. Henderson once said that Bradshaw was so dumb that he couldn't spell cat if you gave him the c and the a, 1996

"I learned quick that at this level the quarterback and the head coach are the two most visible people on the team, and you'd better be on the same page. And if the coach can't find that page, then the coach has a problem . . . With Troy (Aikman), I made the early mistakes, and I learned from that, and it wasn't going to happen here (Miami Dolphins). I treated Troy like I treated quarterbacks in college, and that didn't make for a good first couple of years."
– Miami Dolphins coach and former Dallas coach Jimmy Johnson, 1996

". . . I'm very glad I didn't have to play professionally in Dallas. Reality is so far-fetched from what Cowboys players believe . . . Most NFL players are put on a pedestal. Cowboys are put so high, it seems like they are on another planet."
— Former SMU and New England Patriots running back Craig James on the Cowboys' off-the-field problems, 1996

"There are only two things Dallas has on us: They have pretty cheerleaders and nice uniforms. Other than that, they have no edge on us."
— Green Bay Packers safety LeRoy Butler, 1995

"It's amazing that Jerry Jones can make you feel sorry for old Tom Landry and even kind of sorry for Jimmy Johnson. Even if Dale Carnegie was the coach, it wouldn't help. Ann Landers and Oral Roberts couldn't help the Cowboys, not that they'd want any help. It's amazing to me how fans in Dallas can put up with those guys."
— Mark Nelson, co-author of *The Official Dallas Cowboys Haters Handbook,* 1996

"The Thanksgiving Day game has helped give us our notoriety. Everybody is sitting around eating their turkey and watching the team with the star on the helmet. It's a national tradition. Some people hate us; some people love us. But we're on television. That's the way it is."
— Veteran Dallas Cowboys safety Bill Bates on Dallas' traditional Thanksgiving Day game, 1996

". . . Dallas puts you in a situation where it is almost like minimum wage, like ten or fifteen years from now you have your kids asking, 'Well, why can't you afford to send me to college, Dad?' And I would have to say, 'Well, I decided to play for the Cowboys instead of the 49ers.'"

– Former Cowboys linebacker Ken Norton, Jr., who left Dallas to sign a five-year, $8 million free agent contract with the San Francisco 49ers, 1995

"We're not trying to bring peace to Bosnia or rework the minimum wage. What we're doing is trying to offer a respite to the fans from their hard work on their jobs or whatever personal troubles they might have. We want them to have fun with the Cowboys, and the way to do that is to give them a winning team."
– Jerry Jones

"I'm already emotional about the Dallas game. It would kill me to get beat by them. I'm so angered by the arrogance of the Dallas players and fans—everyone from the owner down to the ball boy."
– Former Green Bay Packers guard Jerry Kramer on the 1996 NFL title game between Dallas and Green Bay

"Michael Jordan is God in tennis shoes and Jerry Rice is God in cleats."
– Dallas Cowboys wide receiver Michael Irvin, 1994

"I think Troy (Aikman) is probably the best quarterback in the league and has been for several years. But it doesn't make any difference whether you have Y.A. Tittle back there. If you have the heat on him, there is no way he can handle it."
– Arizona Cardinals coach Buddy Ryan on his defensive strategy (a few days later, his team lost to Dallas 38-3), 1994

"He (Troy Aikman) has a Michael Jordan mentality. He wants to win. He wants to win in practice. Aikman is very disciplined, and if (offensive coordinator) Ernie Zampese lets him throw the ball forty times a game, he'd break every record in the NFL."
– Roger Staubach, 1996

"Troy (Aikman) is more accurate, and (John) Elway throws it harder. Troy has three Super Bowl rings. Elway has three losses."
– Cowboys wide receiver Anthony Miller, a former Denver Bronco, on the difference between Aikman and Denver quarterback John Elway, 1997

"I told our players that some days you eat the bear, some days the bear eats you. And we ate the bear today."
– Barry Switzer after a 38-3 win over Arizona, 1994

"In my opinion, he's fundamentally the best quarterback that's ever played the game. He's perfect. You cannot find a flaw in his mechanics drop, throwing motion, balance, all that stuff. Nobody's close to him fundamentally. Aikman does everything—and most things better than everybody else."
– Tampa Bay quarterback Trent Dilfer on Troy Aikman, 1997

"We don't let our egos get in the way of the ballclub. We understand that sometimes you have to suppress your own selfish desires to benefit the team. Maybe that is something Jimmy and Jerry never understood and were never capable of understanding."
– Troy Aikman, 1994

"Players win championships; damned coaches don't do it. I don't really believe it really matters to them who their football coach is, as long as they have respect for their system and the way they are treated."
– Barry Switzer, 1994

"I really love the people of Dallas. They know everything about you, and they want to know when you're going to play and what you're going to do. It's a great feeling."
– Deion Sanders, 1995

"It would be hard for me to be a coach, because I would be awfully demanding. Things athletically came naturally to me, and then I worked to improve . . . I think of coaches as being teachers, and I don't know how good I would be because I never really had to be taught a lot of things."
– Troy Aikman, 1996

"I've never seen one sport so dominant as Dallas football. A lot of fans put themselves in the place of the athletes. So the Cowboys have a lot to do with enhancing your self-concept or decreasing your self-concept."
– Dr. Michael Altekruse, chairman of the Department of Counseling, Development and Higher Education at the University of North Texas, 1997

"Success spoils people, especially Cowboys fans in Dallas, Texas. It can be one of the best places in the world to play and one of the worst. The fans become so accustomed to having one of the best franchises of all time. So when things aren't going well, the Cowboys get torn down instead of rallied around."
– Former Cowboys running back Tony Dorsett, 1997

"Thank God there is no Barry Switzer here. I had enough of that rah-rah collegiate stuff when Jimmy (Johnson) was in Dallas, and I didn't want to go through it again. I was just getting used to what Jimmy was doing when he left. Now it's like a baby Jimmy starting all over again."
   – Former Dallas linebacker Ken Norton, Jr., who left to join the
      49ers, 1994

"I found out a long time ago that this is a tough place to play. I've never thought it was a sports town. It's strictly a winner's town. When things are going well, everybody loves you. When they're not, well . . ."
   – Troy Aikman on Dallas fans, 1997

Cowboys Named
Super Bowl MVPs

Super Bowl V, 1971: Chuck Howley
Super Bowl VI, 1972: Roger Staubach
Super Bowl XII, 1978: Randy White, Harvey Martin
Super Bowl XXVII, 1993: Troy Aikman
Super Bowl XXVIII, 1994: Emmitt Smith
Super Bowl XXX, 1996: Larry Brown

"I don't miss the limelight. I'm just more comfortable out of it. Dandy Don is somebody else. He wasn't a bad guy. I have great memories, but I don't miss any of it."
   – Former Dallas Cowboys quarterback Don Meredith, who
      later turned to acting and sports broadcasting, reflecting on
      his career in a rare 1997 interview

"He can motivate the socks right off of you if it's thirty below zero and you don't have a stitch of clothing except a pair of dirty underwear."
  – Former Oklahoma Sooner Brian Bosworth on Barry Switzer,
    1994

"I think he (Barry Switzer) has done awfully well . . . I think if a person was successful in college, they generally become successful in the NFL."
  – Kansas City Chiefs owner Lamar Hunt, 1995

"Unless he is hit by a truck or he's shot, he'll be a part of the Dallas Cowboys for a long time."
  – Dallas Cowboys owner Jerry Jones, on criticism of Switzer, 1995

"Some players leave the game with a handful of money. Some players leave the game with a fistful of rings. I'm a player who wants to leave the game with a handful of money and a fistful of rings."
  – Dallas running back Emmitt Smith, after signing a $12.5
    million contract, 1996

"Emmitt Smith will be with the Dallas Cowboys for as long as he plays football."
  – Jerry Jones, 1996

"When it's all said and done, Emmitt Smith will be one of the greatest who ever played the game. He'll be in the Hall of Fame, and we'll all say we were a part of it, we saw it, and we'll be happy for it."
  – Barry Switzer, 1996

"It's not that I didn't like him. But he didn't have stopwatch speed—4.65. He was undersized, had average hands and left school early. Our mistake was we based the decision too much on the numbers and not enough on performance. He's a great player."
— Tampa Bay personnel director Jerry Angelo on bypassing Emmitt Smith in the pro draft

"Barry (Switzer) just gets teams to win. The fact he's been in the NFL two years with great personnel and been one game away from a Super Bowl and won another Super Bowl basically confirms he's a great coach."
— Jerry Jones, 1996

"Jimmy Johnson put together a great team and a chemistry and established a formula for winning. They're still living with that and will until their great players leave. That is the heritage the Cowboys have now, and sometimes they might win in spite of other people. Is Barry Switzer a major force in this? No, not at all."
— Former San Francisco 49ers coach Bill Walsh, 1996

"We're finally over our Jerryworld adventure. We get to play the games that count now, not just for the owners of the NFL. We got to see Mexico twice. We played in Monterrey and got to see Juarez from a bus."
— Dallas coach Barry Switzer on owner Jerry Jones's pre-season schedule that included five games and three scrimmages in two countries and two states, 1996

"Never in a million years did I think the Dallas Cowboys would be 1-3."
— Deion Sanders after the team's 1-3 start in 1996

"We're a desperate football team. Unless we start playing better, we're in for a long season."
— Barry Switzer, 1996

"We're not able to run the football, and we can't throw the ball."
— Dallas Cowboys quarterback Troy Aikman on the team's struggling offense, 1996

"You gotta score points and touchdowns, and we've not been doing that. It doesn't take Confucius to figure it out . . . Everybody is frustrated. Troy is frustrated. I'm frustrated. If Crazy Ray was here, he'd be frustrated."
— Barry Switzer, 1996

"God put Emmitt Smith here to run with the football."
— Dallas Cowboys wide receiver Michael Irvin, 1994

"I told Troy I wouldn't trade him for any other quarterback in America. He's a champion, but this will hurt him for a long time."
— Barry Switzer, on Aikman's last-minute interception that cost Dallas a victory against Philadelphia, 1996

"My dance was rusty. I haven't been in the end zone in so long that I was off-step and off-beat. Hopefully, I'll get in there some more and we can correct that."
— Dallas Cowboys receiver/cornerback Deion Sanders, after catching a touchdown pass, 1996

"My dream is to be an evangelist. That's my calling. I am Deion Sanders, I am Prime Time. The words I speak go a long way. They go places pastors and bishops can't go."
– Deion Sanders, on his born-again experience, 1997

"I'd rather have Jesus than silver and gold."
– Deion Sanders, 1997

"It's the only stadium that I ever had to leave because I had to go to the bathroom. That happened my first year there. I tried to fake it and act like I was going to see someone."
– Barry Switzer, when asked if he had any special memories of RFK Stadium in Washington, 1996

"I spent five of the best years of my life with Jimmy Johnson. Five great years. It should have been for ten years, but I know we both did what we thought we had to do."
– Jerry Jones, 1996

"I don't miss Jimmy, he wasn't my wife, he was my coach. I don't get into that male bonding."
– Dallas Cowboys guard Nate Newton on former Dallas coach Jimmy Johnson, 1996

"We showed the country that the Dallas Cowboys are a team to be reckoned with. I think that's the best we've played all year. Troy was outstanding. He was a surgeon."
– Barry Switzer after his Cowboys beat the Jimmy Johnson-coached Miami Dolphins, 29-10, 1996

"He thinks he's the only coach who can coach football. He's going to flop here (in Miami). He's a coward. He doesn't say anything to your face. He talks through the press. That, to me, is a coward."
– Dallas Cowboys defensive end Charles Haley on Miami coach Jimmy Johnson, 1996

"Jimmy is a great football coach. No one has said that as many times as I have. He's the whole package."
– Dallas Cowboys owner Jerry Jones, on Miami coach Jimmy Johnson, 1996

"I felt good about the fact that we beat a Jimmy Johnson-coached team. This should provide closure . . . an end to how Jimmy left the Cowboys."
– Jerry Jones, 1996

"As far as football is concerned, Jerry's very, very good. He relied on the people with expertise. I don't want people to think he's meddlesome with personnel and blocking protection. Jerry was very good in that way . . . I've got a lot of respect for Jerry Jones. He's the greatest businessman I've ever known."
– Jimmy Johnson on Jerry Jones, 1996

"You shouldn't be startled by a person who has taken the attitude that football is his god. Jimmy has developed into a personality that, you're the enemy, and you don't deal with the enemy."
– University of Arkansas athletic director Frank Broyles on Jimmy Johnson, 1996

"We have, in our head coach, someone who I think is underestimated in his intellect and is underestimated in his involvement in the

strategy aspect. I don't know how you can criticize his fabulous record. He has won national championships and won a Super Bowl."
– Jerry Jones on Barry Switzer, 1996

"He listens to a different drummer than me as far as lifestyle. But there are things I know about him that are real good. I like him. I'm one of the few who thinks he does a good job."
– Former Brownwood High football coach Gordon Wood, on Barry Switzer, 1997

"The only thing that separates NFL and college teams is that in a college game, if you stop their four or five best plays, you usually have a great shot to win. In professional football, you can stop their four or five best plays, and they'll come out with four or five different plays in the second half. That game-day adjusting is one of the biggest differences between college and pro football."
– Dallas Cowboys defensive coordinator Dave Campo, 1996

"If the Cowboys can pull this season out of the toilet, they deserve a parade."
– Dallas city council member Bob Stimson, 1996

"We may have to have the Police Department help us with some of the floats because some of the players and dignitaries may be riding in paddy wagons."
– Dallas city council member Craig McDaniel discussing the need for a city parade to honor the Cowboys after the playoffs (the team had been hit with seven suspensions for drug violations over a two-year period), 1996

"It was a shock. I kind of felt a little light-headed, like I might faint. I've got a lot of big butterflies and bats flying around in my stomach. It's really an odd feeling."
 – Dallas Cowboys linebacker Jim Schwantz on being selected
   to the Pro Bowl, 1996

"I can't tell you the future. I can just tell you what happened today. I'm not Dionne Warwick and I don't know the number for the psychic hotline."
 – Dallas Cowboys wide receiver Michael Irvin after a 38-20 loss
   to San Francisco, 1995

"There is just no need to have longer agreements or extended obligations unless it is necessary to get the job done. But I want to reiterate that apart from doing the right thing financially for the club, my personal feelings are that he will be coaching the Dallas Cowboys for many years to come."
 – Jerry Jones on Barry Switzer, 1996

"It was a low 2-iron with a duck hook on it that should have been blocked up the middle. You don't want to hit them like that."
 – Barry Switzer on Danny Kight's 34-yard field goal (it was
   good) in a pre-season game, 1997

"It's like Pearl Harbor every week. It's a surprise attack. You don't know what you're going to get until you get in there."
 – Barry Switzer on the opposition's blitzing packages, 1997

"Between the twenty-yard lines we're the best team in the NFL."
 – Emmitt Smith referring to the fact the Cowboys were the
   worst team at scoring touchdowns once they penetrated the
   twenty-yard line, 1997

"I don't have any knowledge of him being the subject of any type of inquiry. This could not happen without Leon, me or someone in the organization knowing about it."
– Cowboys owner Jerry Jones shortly before Dallas defensive lineman Leon Lett was suspended for drug use by the NFL, 1996

"This organization was built by people with great moral character. You try to uphold that. But we have tarnished the organization some with a string of incidents, and it's unfortunate."
– Dallas Cowboys fullback Daryl Johnston, 1997

"Having gone to college in Los Angeles and having been a pretty high-profile player, nothing could have prepared me for life in Dallas when you are the Cowboys quarterback. I had to grow up in a hurry."
– Troy Aikman

"If you are a star on this team in Dallas, Texas, it's like being Tom Cruise or Leonardo DiCaprio in Los Angeles. You can own the town. Of course, it can be a blessing or a curse."
– Michael Irvin

"Everyone is responsible for their own behavior and decisions, and it ain't going to be whether your mama or daddy or coach had any influence."
– Barry Switzer, 1997

"These guys have had a thousand do-good talks from high school and college coaches. It boils down to those people finally accepting the responsibility to do the right things."
– Barry Switzer on the team's off-the-field problems, 1997

"I think the kids really listened this off-season, and they made the decision to stay out of trouble."
  – Barry Switzer on the Cowboys' lack of off-the-field problems in 1997

"You weigh the whole player, not just the character issue. You obviously don't want an ax murderer on your team, but you take everything into account on an individual basis."
  – Dallas Cowboys coach Chan Gailey

"This franchise has to be very careful. Fame is a microscope, but Dallas Cowboy fame is an electron microscope. You've always got to keep that in mind."
  – Calvin Hill, hired by Jerry Jones to serve as the team's behavioral consultant

"Rerun it, rewrite it, reprint it. Just like you did, with the same intensity that you did—the same intensity. Don't lose the intensity. Don't lose the intensity."
  – Cowboys wide receiver Michael Irvin to reporters after he was cleared of wrongdoing in a sexual assault investigation, 1997

"Kendell's not an angel, but that's not a tabernacle choir they've got in Dallas."
  – Sports agent Brian Levy, whose client Kendell Watkins was released by Dallas for off-the-field behavior, 1997

"It's the egotism of the Cowboys. The biggest thing they stole was the title of America's Team. We really believe we're America's Team. If the Cowboys represent what America is all about, we're in deep trouble."
  – Green Bay Packers public address announcer Gary Knafelc, 1997

"Team turmoil. South America's Team. The Chaotic Cowboys. Choose one. Choose all of the above. Choose none of the above . . . Even in football-crazy Texas, where the Cowboys are worshipped, enough seems to be enough."
— Boston Globe columnist Mark Blaudschun, 1997

"They have been called America's Team. They also have been called America's Most Wanted . . . A team you might take home to Mom if she were Ma Barker."
— Baltimore Sun columnist Vito Stellino, 1997

> **"There has never been a period, at any point in Cowboy history, when everybody was an angel."**
> **— Daryl Johnston**

"Say what you want about Dallas. The Cowboys believe in forgiveness. Loyalty. Outside of murder, you can't do too much wrong on this team."
— Nate Newton, on the return to the team of troubled wide receiver Michael Irvin, 1996

"If I was Jerry Jones, I'd have an entire wing at Betty Ford (treatment center) just for the Cowboys. I think history tells us it has been a team that needs an entire wing."
— Thomas "Hollywood" Henderson, 1997

"You know what team spends the most money on its players? The Dallas Cowboys . . . and that's just bail money."
— Comedian Jay Leno, "The Tonight Show"

"Whenever I see the Cowboys on TV, I don't know who to root for—the defense or the prosecution. No, this will never be America's Team. If it is, then woe for America."
– Former Green Bay guard Jerry Kramer

"I'm looking forward to taking over my ranch from Dad and having my Mom make coconut cream pies."
– Cowboys tight end Jay Novacek on his retirement plans, 1997

"I played with all my heart and in pain because I loved the game."
– Dallas Cowboys defensive lineman Charles Haley, announcing his retirement, 1997

"This league can't survive without the Cowboys. We need to be in the drama somewhere."
– Cowboys offensive guard Nate Newton, on the Cowboys' struggles to make the playoffs, 1997

"What do you want me to do, take him out and shoot him?"
– Barry Switzer, when asked what he would do about running back Sherman Williams' problem of fumbling. Earlier the same day, Switzer pled guilty to a misdemeanor charge of carrying a gun without a permit, 1997

"I got lots of calls. People either like him or really hate him. Some thought his case should be dismissed and he get an apology. Others wanted him to go to the penitentiary, and that's not even in the law."
– Tarrant County Criminal Court Judge Daryl Coffey, after sentencing Switzer to perform eighty hours of community service and fining him $3,500 on a misdemeanor gun charge

"They still have what I call the Holy Trinity in Aikman, Smith and Irvin, so I'm not counting them out because they've struggled a little this season."
– Green Bay quarterback Brett Favre, 1997

· "We got beat. We got beat bad. The last time I took a beating like that, my father gave it to me."
– Cowboys wide receiver Michael Irvin after a 45-17 loss to Green Bay, 1997

"Our coaching staff should take a significant part of the blame for the loss. If we had a chance, we'd do some things all over again coaching-wise. Watching films today was an embarrassment. We should have made some adjustments."
– Jerry Jones after the Green Bay loss, 1997

"If Jerry (Jones) wants to make a change, he'll make that decision. If I want to coach here, I'll make that decision. There's only two of us involved and we're the only two that matter . . . it never enters my mind. I don't even think about it. It's irrelevant."
– Embattled Dallas coach Barry Switzer, 1997

"Why would I watch my back? Jerry's already told me that if I go, (the assistants) go. Ain't none of them going to be the head coach . . . Nobody has been disloyal, but if anybody stabs me in the back, they're not going to be here. They're not going to be with the Dallas Cowboys and certainly not considered for the head coaching position."
– Barry Switzer, 1997

"When Jerry sees fit for him to leave, he'll leave. Until that time comes, let Barry do his job."
– Emmitt Smith, 1997

"I might want to travel to Europe, get on my Harley and go . . . wherever. This is all I've done for forty years. I don't want to coach anywhere else. If I don't coach here next year, I'll just be a fan. I'll do things with my family and kids. That's more important, anyway."
— Barry Switzer, 1997

"We played a pretty good ballgame other than the second and third quarters."
— Troy Aikman after a loss to Cincinnati, 1997

"The Cowboys get everyone's best game. It's like playing the New York Rangers in hockey or the Yankees in baseball. You want to give your best against America's Team."
— Cincinnati quarterback Boomer Esiason, 1997

"There will be a lot of changes. It got ugly today. I told Jerry he ought to get rid of the whole damn bunch of us."
— Barry Switzer, after a season-ending 20-7 loss to the New York Giants, 1997

"I feel bad for the fans. In light of the way we've played this year, I was surprised as many of them stayed as long as they did today."
— Troy Aikman after the loss to the Giants, 1997

"There's only one guy who can answer that for you, and that would be Jerry Jones. I haven't pulled the trigger yet. He's got the gun, but I might take it from him.
— Barry Switzer, on speculation he would be fired

"Ever since I've been aware of sports and athletics, Barry Switzer has been a part of my consciousness. Where I come from (Arkansas) that's just the way things were. It's a personal thing with me."
– Jerry Jones, 1997

**"Without being overly optimistic,
I can see Chan Gailey coaching the team
ten years from now."**
– Jerry Jones, 1998

"In March of 1994, Barry Switzer was the right person to take on this challenge . . . When you consider Barry is one of just seventeen men in history who have brought home that Super Bowl trophy, his ledger is square with me."
– Jerry Jones, announcing Switzer's forced resignation, 1998

"It probably would have been best if I had encouraged Barry (Switzer) to leave after we won the Super Bowl. But he never got the credit for the job he did."
– Jerry Jones, 1999

"The guy I'm talking to will jazz you. He's different from Jimmy (Johnson) and Barry (Switzer), he'll put a tingle in you."
– Jerry Jones, on interviewing Green Bay assistant Sherman Lewis for the Dallas head coaching job

"I'm personally responsible for what's happened. I've always said it all starts with the head coach and goes down from there."
– Barry Switzer

"The only thing we're not going to do is use the Wishbone or the Run and Shoot. We're going to do whatever it takes to move the ball, whether it's a double reverse or a pass off the double reverse."
– Chan Gailey

"The process began with an image in my mind. I'm proud it took so long. I gave this club, our players and our fans the opportunity to end up with the best man. Chan's the man."
– Jerry Jones, on hiring Chan Gailey to replace Switzer

"I think the way he (Gailey) coaches will be a lot like the way Coach Landry coached. I see the way his meetings are run on time, and there's no lollygagging. That's the way Coach Landry ran his meetings."
– Bill Bates

"I have no idea. I wish we could just huddle in the corner of the end zone like we did in Pop Warner football. Because whatever happens in the locker room is unbelievable. I wish we could just huddle, get our Hershey bar like we did in Pee Wee football and go from there."
– Deion Sanders, on the team's struggles in the second half of games, 1999

"It was the same thing I tell them most of the time. 'Let's go.' There wasn't any great Knute Rockne speech on the sidelines before we went out on the field. We just went out and tried to execute."
– Chan Gailey after his team overcame a twenty-one-point halftime deficit to beat Washington, 1999

"I've never been on a team yet that didn't need more speed. You always take more speed. But if we go out and sign the 400-meter relay team . . . that doesn't make us a better football team."
 – Chan Gailey

"It's as if the Grim Reaper is walking our sidelines. I've seen seasons like this before. We've got a tough situation. I certainly don't have the answers."
 – Cowboys scouting director Larry Lacewell, after the team
    started 4-4 and suffered numerous injuries in 1999

"There's no way we can ever have a season like this and not make changes. I feel the way I feel when I drill a dry hole in the oil and gas business."
 – Jerry Jones, in the midst of an 8-8 season in 1999

"Dallas doesn't deserve to be in the playoffs. Sometimes when you aren't playing well, it means you're not paying attention to detail. I think that's one of the things that just shows the Cowboys problem is that they aren't a good team. They aren't the same Cowboys anymore."
 – TV football analyst John Madden on the 1999 Cowboys

"My relationship with the Cowboys hasn't been good. You have to admire the way they brought in the talent to win the Super Bowls. Getting Jimmy (Johnson) was a big key. If Tom (Landry) had retired, Jimmy would have been one of my top picks."
 – Former Cowboys president-general manager Tex Schramm in
    1999

"When we talk about what we're going to be doing this week, next week and next year . . . every bit of that is with the thought that Chan (Gailey) is going to be our coach."
– Jerry Jones, shortly before firing Gailey, 2000

"I'm a big fan of Chan. I think he'll bring back the discipline there."
– Philadelphia Eagles coach Ray Rhodes

"This decision I had to make is about football. It wasn't about egos. It wasn't about contentiousness. Chan Gailey, relative to when he accepted this job, burned the midnight oil. He worked hard, he was diligent, he was honest. He did everything I imagined."
– Jerry Jones on firing Gailey after the coach posted an 18-16 record in two seasons

"(Jerry Jones) should go ahead and name himself the head coach, then go get an offensive coordinator. Whether he calls himself that or not, Jerry is already the head coach of the Cowboys. He allows players to come to him, he gives them motivational speeches, and (Chan) Gailey was essentially just his offensive coordinator."
– Former SMU and New England coach Ron Meyer, 2000

"I had two good years in Dallas. We'll leave it at that."
– Former Dallas head coach Chan Gailey after being named offensive coordinator of the Miami Dolphins, 2000

OVERTIME
Tuna Takes Charge (2000s)

Following the dismissal of Chan Gailey, Cowboys owner Jerry Jones found himself in a dilemma. Jones's reputation as a hands-on, interfering owner made it difficult for him to attract a proven coach to take over the team.

With that in mind, Jones opted to promote veteran defensive coordinator Dave Campo to the top spot in 2000. Campo's tenure was marked by the release of star quarterback Troy Aikman and a dismal three-year record of 15-33, composed of three consecutive 5-11 seasons.

In what was becoming a habit, Jones, facing mounting criticism, fired Campo following the 2002 season.

On January 2, 2003, Bill Parcells became the sixth coach in team history. To entice the highly-successful Parcells out of retirement and to Dallas, Jones promised to give the new coach more control of the team and to work together for the overall benefit of the franchise. Prior to taking the Dallas job, Parcells had accumulated a career record of 149 -106 -1, including two Super Bowl victories with the New York Giants and another Super Bowl appearance with the New England Patriots.

Parcells earned the nickname "Tuna" in 1980 while he was an assistant coach with the Patriots. A player or group of players approached Parcells with a nonsensical request, to which Parcells replied, "Who do you think I am? Charlie the Tuna?"

Parcells' no-nonsense approach was well-accepted by ownership, players, and fans. In his first season, the Cowboys rebounded to post a 10 - 6 record and advanced to the first round of the playoffs before losing.

The 2004 season did not prove to be as successful. In a surprise move that was never publicly explained, the Cowboys cut starting quarterback Quincy Carter in training camp. Led by forty-year-old quarterback Vinny Testaverde, the club struggled to a 6-10 record.

With veteran quarterback Drew Bledsoe firmly entrenched as the starter in 2005, Dallas regained its winning ways with a 9-7 mark, but losses in several key games down the stretch kept them out of the playoffs. Rumors began to swirl that the aging Parcells would retire, but he signed a new contract after the season.

After playing in the Cotton Bowl and Texas Stadium, the Cowboys began making plans to move into a brand-new state-of-the-art stadium in Arlington in 2009. A potential agreement between the City of Dallas and the Cowboys to bring the team back to Fair Park to a new facility to replace the Cotton Bowl ultimately fell through. Arlington voters approved a new stadium in November 2004.

* * *

"About the only difference is that he's dressing a lot better."
– Safety Darren Woodson, on the change in Dave Campo since he was promoted from defensive coordinator to head coach

"When you get blown out the way we did, everything is bad. The water is nasty. The towels don't smell good. The showers don't feel

warm. If there was a word for the way we played, you couldn't write it."
  – Emmitt Smith, after a 41-14 loss to Philadelphia, 2000

"Troy will always be a Dallas Cowboy. When people look at him, they will always see him with a star on the side of his helmet."
  – Jerry Jones after the Cowboys released quarterback Troy Aikman in 2001

"I was the last one (of the Triplets) to come, but that doesn't mean I had to be the last one to go. That's not the way I would have written the script. I would have written a happy ending. You know, most stories about Cowboys have happy endings."
  – Emmitt Smith on Aikman's release

"That doesn't bother me. The name of the game is winning, especially in Dallas, Texas. We have a tremendous tradition here for winning. That doesn't surprise me at all, and I really don't focus on any of that. The only thing I focus on is the next football game, and I have a real good relationship with this organization, and certainly all decisions that are made as far as who is hired and fired, what we're going to do, how we're going to do it, how we're going to scout all of those things are made in the best of intentions for the Cowboys to win. So I'm not worried about anything other than the Tennessee Titans right now."
  – Dave Campo, on rumors of his upcoming dismissal

"This change is more about a change in philosophy—not about what Dave (Campo) didn't do. Dave was hired because he represented a continuation of philosophy. The philosophy that we have had was a winning philosophy that produced three world championships."
  – Jerry Jones, on firing Dave Campo in 2002

"When I accepted this position, I didn't take it with a disclaimer that said things wouldn't be difficult. I knew what I was getting into. I knew that we were an organization in transition. I knew that there would be strong challenges. I truly love this organization, love this community, the Jones family and the passion they have for the game of football and the Dallas Cowboys. I'm a Dallas Cowboy, and part of me will always be a Dallas Cowboy."
– Dave Campo, after being fired, 2003

"It's good people, solid people here. There's a real Mayberry R.F.D. feel to it, and that's nice. People out here want to have good, clean fun."
– Nate Newton, on training camp in Wichita Falls

**"The Cowboys are good for Texas.
They uplift the psyche of the state.
People feel better when they're winning.
It brings out Texas pride."**
– Texas Gov. George W. Bush

"I'm excited about creating the capacity, I want 100,000 seats. I want this to be a venue that speaks for what the Cowboys are. We have the franchise that both nationally and internationally can be identified with the Coliseum of Rome."
– Jerry Jones on the prospects of a new stadium, 2000

"I think that star on the helmet was the reason that Dwyane left the scene of the wreck, and that's what so greatly compounded his problems with the law. It's that star that makes those Cowboys feel

so conspicuous—because they are conspicuous. And the star, believe me, doesn't bring any special favors with the law in this town . . . If Goodrich had been some plumber from Garland, he'd have gotten fairer treatment from the DA's office."
   – Anonymous Dallas defender, on teammate-cornerback Dwyane Goodrich, who was arrested for running over and killing two people with his vehicle on LBJ Freeway, 2003

"I am fired up. I don't want to be over in the lounge show, I want to play the big room. That's where Elvis played. That's what the Cowboys are, the big room."
– Dallas Cowboys head coach Bill Parcells

"Let's see how much Parcells wins this year. I'll make him pay when we play them. The homo."
   – New York Giants tight end Jeremy Shockey on former Giants coach Bill Parcells, who had criticized Shockey's play as a TV commentator in 2002, *New York* magazine, Aug. 7, 2003

"I really don't want to comment on something that's just not true. I'm 100 percent sure I didn't say that . . . I think he (the writer) got it mixed up from something my friend may have called him (Parcells)."
   – Jeremy Shockey, denying the "homo' quote, Aug. 8, 2003, *New York Daily News*

"I want to own the Cowboys for the rest of my life. I want to manage the Cowboys for the rest of my life. And when I die, I expect my family to manage the team."
   – Jerry Jones

"I've got two guys (assistant coaches), Sean Payton and Mike Zimmer, you got to keep an eye on those two. Because they are going to try to get the upper hand. Mike wants the defense to do well, and Sean, he is going to have a few, no disrespect to the Orientals, but what we call Jap plays, OK. Surprise things and oh . . . No disrepect to anyone. But you have to watch (Payton and Zimmer) because they will sabotage each other."
– Dallas Cowboys head coach Bill Parcells, at a press conference, June 7, 2004

"Today, during my news conference, I made a very inappropriate reference, and although I prefaced it with the remarks 'no disrespect to anyone intended,' it was still uncalled for and inconsiderate. For that, I apologize to anyone who may have been offended."
– Bill Parcells, on his reference to Orientals

"The quarterback is in charge of the chuck wagon. He's handing it out here and there, but he can't just throw it out there indiscriminately or the wolves will get him."
– Bill Parcells

"I don't like celebrity quarterbacks. We don't need those. We need battlefield commanders."
– Bill Parcells

"This isn't going to be a simple, overnight, one-stop-does-all process. This isn't like driving into the Texaco station, where you tell the guy to change the plugs and adjust the brakes."
– Bill Parcells, on rebuilding the team, even after the 10-6

record of 2003

"History doesn't mean anything in football; history means something in boxing."

– Bill Parcells

"Years from now when we're looking at the history of the Cowboys, I want to be known as someone who did everything we could to have success. The way fans felt about the people who brought Babe Ruth to the Yankees . . . "

– Jerry Jones

"You have to clean his cage in the morning, feed him some seed, get him some water, put him on a swing and let him swing back and forth, put his shade up and see if he's all right."

– Bill Parcells, comparing the injured Darren Woodson to a pet
parakeet. Woodson's schedule included riding a bike and
eating as he could not practice, 2004

**"I tell the players we are in a replacement
business. I replaced somebody. Jerry replaced
somebody. And someone is going to replace us.
I learned that a long time ago."**
– Bill Parcells, on how he deals with players

"He needs to go down to Ace Hardware and get a little Rust-Oleum."

– Bill Parcells on receiver Keyshawn Johnson, who was rusty in
pre-season after missing the last six games of the 2003 season, 2004

"He's matured a great deal. He's not the same young man he was two or three years ago . . . He takes a lot more responsibility for what happens to him, and he recognizes that he controls his destiny."
  – Jerry Jones, four days before releasing starting quarterback
    Quincy Carter

"I would say that he's got a leg up because he played here last year, and so I have that in my mind. If someone was to completely outperform him . . . you can't fool the players. They know who can do it. But he's in good position to be improved, and he should be improved."
  – Bill Parcells, before releasing Quincy Carter

"This is a tough result for our team and for him as an individual. Quincy did some really good things while he was there. But there are some things that having imperfections in, those don't fit with the team concept."
  – Dallas owner Jerry Jones on the release of Quincy Carter

"I want you to know—on my part—that this was not a difficult decision at all. It is, though, very disappointing. Very disappointing."
  – Jerry Jones on Carter's release

"This is not something that came up last night or the night before last night. Jerry knows what he was getting when he got someone like me. We talked about what kinds of players I want on my team. What kind of group I want to try to put together."
  – Bill Parcells on Carter's release

"Everybody's ready to put him in the cemetery. I'm trying to dig him up."
> — Parcells, on his forty-year-old starting quarterback Vinny Testaverde, 2004

"We don't have a chance right now. This is definitely the low point of my time here in Dallas. I'm embarrassed to put a team on the field that looks like that . . . If we don't play better defense, we don't have a chance to win another game."
> — Cowboys coach Bill Parcells, after a 41-20 loss at Green Bay, 2004

"Everybody wants to bury us and wax up the hearses and order plenty of flowers. That's not what we're thinking."
> — Dallas Cowboys wide receiver Keyshawn Johnson, after the Cowboys' 2-4 start in 2004

"It's like an old car in the winter. You know the car is a good car. It's been there for you for years. Then you crank it up and it doesn't quite turn over, but once it does turn over, the heat comes on and everything is up and great again."
> — Dallas Cowboys kicker Richie Anderson on the team's slow start

"We're too stupid. I can't put anything in their hands . . . I'm ashamed of myself and my team."
> — Dallas Cowboys coach Bill Parcells, after his team was upset by the Cincinnati Bengals, 26-3, 2004

"You get a little down and out once in awhile, but I didn't think about quitting. I didn't think about quitting. I just wouldn't do it."
> — Bill Parcells, after a frustrating 2004 season

"We took a bad beating tonight. We have to get back to work. I'm not going to get into the state of the union tonight, and I'm not going to give you any sound bites."
– Bill Parcells, to the media after a 49-21 home loss to the Eagles, 2004

Dallas Cowboys Training Camps

1960: Pacific University, Forest Grove, Oregon
1961: St. Olaf, Northfield, Minnesota
1962: Northern Michigan College, Marquette, Michigan
1963-89: Cal Lutheran College, Thousand Oaks, California
1990-97: St. Edward's University, Austin, Texas
1998-01: Midwestern State University, Wichita Falls, Texas
2002-03: Alamodome, San Antonio, Texas
2004-06: Oxnard, California

"One week, we show positive signs. The next week, we look like a team that hasn't even been coached. Going through a season like we're going through now, it's like walking into the mob when you walk into this building. It's a dreadful place to be."
– Dallas Cowboys linebacker Dexter Coakley, in the midst of a 6-10 season, 2004

"I know we get along well. We're making decisions in a healthy way with good debate, and all of that is working a lot better than most people thought it would."
– Jerry Jones, on his relationship with Bill Parcells, 2005

"I know we don't have any Dallas people here. They're the ugliest people in the world."
- Washington Redskins coach Joe Gibbs, during Fan Appreciation Day at Redskins Park, August 6, 2005

"At our fan day, I kind of got caught up in things there and obviously somebody was yelling some things about the Cowboys and I tried to make a joke. I was joking. I was joking. It didn't come out probably like a joke like it should've."
- Joe Gibbs, apologizing for his "ugly" Dallas remarks, August 7, 2005

"Well, he's got a little Patton in him, doesn't he? . . . Parcells has proven his approbation means everything to these guys. He's a real coach in the pantheon with Lombardi and Walsh and Noll and Landry."
- Comedian/commentator Dennis Miller, after visiting a Dallas workout

Home Field Advantage

1960-70: Cotton Bowl, Dallas, Texas
1971-present: Texas Stadium, Irving, Texas

"Well, if you want to spend $18,000, you can break it. If it's worth it, take me with you."
- Bill Parcells on the fine for players missing his curfew

"Don't put him in Canton (NFL Hall of Fame) yet."
– Bill Parcells, after an outstanding pre-season game performance by rookie DeMarcus Ware, 2005

"The kid will run. He will block. He will catch. I'm not saying he's
going to be Gale Sayers. But he has ability in all the areas that are
prerequisites."
– Cowboys coach Bill Parcells on rookie running back Marion
Barber, who rushed for 127 yards and two touchdowns in a
34-13 win over Arizona, 2005

"He's thick, but he has to lose a little weight. We're not playing
Chubby Checker out there. I know what his former coach had him
play at, so we're going with that."
– Bill Parcells on rookie defensive tackle Marcus Spears, 2005

"When you play this position and things are going well, everything's groovy and they all want to talk about you. When it's not
going well, you're the first one they throw under the bus."
– Dallas quarterback Drew Bledsoe, on his thirteen-year career
in the NFL

"This is funny. The media thinks you can just dial 1-800 and get
a quarterback. There are teams that have been trying to dial that
for ten years. They think you can just dial it up. You think we don't
look around? You think, 'Well, you've got to get a quarterback.' No
(kidding). You act like someone is not trying to."
– Bill Parcells to the media on the perception that it is easy to
sign a quality NFL quarterback

"Practice was superior today compared to yesterday . . . it would've been hard to be worse than that. Roosevelt Junior High could've played better than yesterday."
– Parcells, on a lackluster workout, 2005

"This is a mechanical job. You have to be able to execute the mechanics of this job. It's a zero-tolerance thing. That's the best way I can put it. It requires perfection or almost perfection. If you can't come close enough to that, then things are going to change."
– Parcells on the struggles of rookie deep snapper Jon Condo

"There's a pressure to perform at a high level. Some people can handle it, and some people can't. Parcells finds out who can't, and they're removed."
– Dallas nose tackle La'Roi Glover

"Maybe I shouldn't have done it exactly the way I did. But I'd already said it about fifty seconds before. I told him to stop, and he didn't, so I thought I needed to get his attention. So that's what happened, and I don't care what anyone thinks."
– Parcells, on shoving his wide receivers coach Todd Haley on the sideline during a game against Seattle. Haley continued to shout at an official as Parcells was talking to the official.

"I saw frustration, I saw a ticked-off coach, and that's better than anything I've felt during my seven years in the NFL. I wanted this one bad. To see the look on Bill Parcells' face walking off the field, that's all the Thanksgiving I need. I don't need no turkey tonight."
– Denver Broncos defensive lineman Ebenezer Ekuban after Denver beat Dallas 24-21 in overtime on Thanksgiving. Ekuban was released by the Cowboys in 2003.

"In Texas, Thanksgiving dinner is scheduled around football. We ruined a whole bunch of appetites. A lot of people in Texas are sick. They don't want their dessert. No pumpkin pie, no sweet potato pie for them."

    – Denver rookie Darrent Williams, on the Broncos' win over Dallas at Texas Stadium

"Football in Texas is like air. You breathe it. These people need it to live. As a kid, I always pictured myself playing for the Cowboys. I was Deion Sanders, playing cornerback, returning kicks. To come in here and get a victory on Thanksgiving? With the whole NFL world watching? That's good, real good, better than a dream."

    – Darrent Williams

"I can play until I'm seventy. What I do doesn't require me to be in a blazer. Terry (Glenn) can play till he's seventy. We don't need to get no (expletive) receiver. You're only as good as the opportunities you get."

    – Dallas Cowboys wide receiver Keyshawn Johnson, age thirty-three, when asked if the team needed a younger receiver

"He was knowledgeable about the defense and called the defense. We would fuss every once in a while, and Coach Landry would tell us to behave. It was a good working relationship, and I'll miss him."

    – Former Cowboys assistant coach Gene Stallings after the death of former Dallas assistant Ernie Stautner

"This is America's Team. I feel right at home. I'm a star among stars . . . Get your popcorn ready. It's going to be a show."

    – Controversial wide receiver Terrell Owens, on signing a three-year, $25 million contract with the Dallas Cowboys in 2006

"I say, 'support it,' and that's the way we go. I don't view it as a gamble. It's in my best interest that he's successful. And it's in his best interest that he's successful."
– Bill Parcells on the acquisition of Terrell Owens

"Jerry (Jones) loves the pop. He loves the hype. I guess you could've gotten more hype if you'd signed Charlie Manson, but I can't think of anyone else that would give you that type of hit."
– Former Cowboys director of scouting Larry Lacewell, on the signing of Terrell Owens and team owner Jerry Jones' thirst for media coverage

"I am thankful to the Dallas Cowboys for giving me a lot of enjoyment the past years."
– A convicted Texas murderer shortly before his execution in Huntsville, 1997

"That is all I have to say, warden . . . Oh, I would like to say in closing—What About Those Cowboys!"
– Inmate William Davis' last words before he was executed in Huntsville, 2000

ACKNOWLEDGMENTS

I wish to thank a number of individuals for their assistance in completing *Dallas Cowboys Quips and Quotes.* For the author, this book has been an "off-and-on" project for about 10 years.

Thanks go to my parents, Bob and Mae Burton of Sherman, for those memorable trips to the Cotton Bowl. Ditto to my old basketball buddy George Olson at the city of Sherman and Betty Roberts of the Sherman Ex-Students Association for research assistance, and Ronnie Perry of Sherman, who opened his vast archives of sports memorabilia to me. Thanks are also in order to Don Eldredge of the *Herald Democrat,* Jack Windlow at A-1 Printing in Sherman and Jason Hicks and Dan Hoke at Southeastern Oklahoma State University in Durant, Oklahoma, for technical support.

I greatly appreciate the cooperation of Rich Dalrymple and the Dallas Cowboys for their permission to publish the photos from my personal collection.

Thanks to Glenn Dromgoole, Carlyn Kahl, and everyone at State House Press for their support of *Dallas Cowboys Quips and Quotes.*

Finally, I want to thank the two most important people in my life and also the two smartest people I know—my wife Michelle and daughter Katie.

BIBLIOGRAPHY

Books

Bayless, Skip. *God's Coach: The Hymns, Hype, & Hypocrisy of Tom Landry's Cowboys.* New York: Simon & Schuster, 1991.

Bayless, Skip. *Hell-Bent: The Crazy Truth About the "Win or Else" Dallas Cowboys.* New York: Harper-Collins Publishers, 1996.

Bayless, Skip. *The Boys: The Untold Story of the Dallas Cowboys' Season on the Edge.* New York: Simon & Schuster, 1993.

Blair, Sam. *Dallas Cowboys: Pro or Con?: A Complete History.* Garden City, NY: Doubleday, 1970.

Cawthorn, Todd. *Jerry Jones and the "New Regime."* Irving, TX: Thorn Publishing, 1995.

Chapman, Donald, Randolph Campbell, and Robert Calvert. *The Dallas Cowboys and the NFL.* Norman, OK: University of Oklahoma Press, 1970.

Chieger, Bob and Pat Sullivan. *Football's Greatest Quotes.* New York: Simon & Schuster, 1990.

Coffey, Frank and Ernie Wood with Tony Seidl. *How 'Bout Them Cowboys!: An In-Depth Look at America's Team the Dallas Cowboys.* Dallas: Taylor Publishing, 1993.

The Dallas Cowboys Media Guides: 1960-2005.

Dallas Cowboys Wives. *The Dallas Cowboys Family "Playbook": A Collection of Recipes, Family Photos, Personal Quotes, Statistics & Trivia!* Dallas: TPG, Inc., 1997.

Dent, Jim. *King of the Cowboys: The Life and Times of Jerry Jones.* Holbrook, MA: Adams Publishing, 1995.

Donovan, Jim, Ken Sims, and Frank Coffey. *The Dallas Cowboys Encyclopedia: The Ultimate Guide to America's Team.* Secaucus, NJ: Carroll Publishing Group, 1996.

Eisenberg, John. *Cotton Bowl Days: Growing Up with Dallas and the Cowboys in the 1960s.* New York: Simon & Schuster, 1997.

Field, Bobbi. *The Dallas Cowboys' Super Wives.* Austin: Shoal Creek, 1972.

Fisher, Mike. *Stars & Strife.* Fort Worth: The Summit Group, 1993.

Garrison, Walt and John Tullius. *Once a Cowboy.* New York: Random House, 1988.

Gent, Pete. *North Dallas Forty.*

Golenbock, Peter. *Cowboys Have Always Been My Heroes: The Definitive Oral History of America's Team.* New York: Warner Books, 1997.

Green, Lee. *Sportswit.* New York: Ballantine Books, 1986.

Harris, Cliff and Charlie Waters. *Tales from the Dallas Cowboys—A Collection of the Greatest Stories Ever Told.* Sports Publishing L.L.C, 2003.

Hayes, Bob with Robert Pack. *Run, Bullet, Run.* New York: Harper & Row, 1990.

Henderson, Thomas "Hollywood" and Peter Knobler. *Out of Control: Confessions of an NFL Casualty.* New York: Putnam, 1987.

Holmes, Michael. *Mamas Don't Let Your Cowboys Grow Up to Be Babies.* ECW Press, Toronto, Ontario, 1998.

Jensen, Brian. *Where Have All Our Cowboys Gone?* New York: Cooper Square Press, 2001.

Johnson, Jimmy with Ed Hinton. *Turning the Thing Around: Pulling America's Team Out of the Dumps—and Myself Out of the Doghouse.* New York: Hyperion, 1993.

Klein, Dave. *Tom and the 'Boys.* New York: Zebra Books, 1990.

Liebman, Glenn. *Sports Shorts.* Chicago: Contemporary Books, 1993.

Lilly, Bob with Sam Blair. *Bob Lilly: Reflections: The Birth of America's Team as seen through the camera of the Dallas Cowboys' first Hall of Fame player.* Dallas: Taylor Publishing, 1983.

Martin, Harvey. *Texas Thunder: My Eleven Years with the Dallas Cowboys.* New York: Rawson Associates, 1986.

Nelson, Mark and Miller Bonner. *The Semi-Official Dallas Cowboys' Haters Handbook.* New York: Collier Books, 1984.

Perkins, Steve. *The Drive to Win: The Making of the Dallas Cowboys.* New York: Tempo Books, 1973.

Perkins, Steve. *Next Year's Champions.* New York: Word Publishing, 1969.

Perkins, Steve. *The Official Dallas Cowboys Bluebook VIII.* Dallas: Taylor Publishing, 1987.

Reid, Jan. *Vain Glory.* Fredericksburg, TX: Shearer, 1986.

Rentzel, Lance. *When All the Laughter Died in Sorrow.* New York: Bantam Books, 1973.

Scholz, Suzette, Stephanie Scholz and Sheri Scholz. *Deep In the Heart of Texas.* New York: St. Martin's Paperbacks, 1991.

Sham, Brad. *Dallas Cowboys Stadium Stories.* Guilford, CT: The Globe Pequot Press, 2003.

Shropshire, Mike. *When the Tuna Went Down to Texas: How Bill Parcells Led the Cowboys Back to the Promised Land.* New York: William Morrow, 2004.

Spagnola, Mickey, et al. *America's Rivalry: The 20 Greatest Redskins-Cowboys Games.* 21st Century Online Publishing, 1997.

Sports Illustrated. They Said It! New York: Oxmoor House, 1990.

St. John, Bob. *Landry: The Man Inside.* Waco: Word Books, 1979.

St. John, Bob. *The Landry Legend.* Waco: Word Books, 1990.

St. John, Bob. *Tex!: The Man Who Built the Dallas Cowboys.* Englewood Cliffs, NJ: Prentice Hall, 1988.

St. John, Bob. *We Love You Cowboys.* New York: Sport Magazine Press, 1972.

Stamborski, Jim. *J.J. Straight Talking: Jimmy Johnson's Insights, Outbursts, Kudos, and Comebacks.* Hollywood, FL: Lifetime Books, 1998.

Staubach, Roger, with Sam Blair and Bob St. John. *First Down, Lifetime to Go.* Waco: Word Books, 1974.

Staubach, Roger, with Frank Luksa. *Time Enough to Win.* Waco: Word Books, 1980.

Stowers, Carlton. *The Cowboy Chronicles.* Austin: Eakin Press, 1984.

Stratton, Gary and Robert Krug. *Dallas Cowboys Trivia Challenge.* Dallas: Taylor Publishing, 1986.

Sugar, Bert, ed. *I Hate the Dallas Cowboys: And Who Elected Them America's Team Anyway?* New York: St. Martin's, 1997.

Switzer, Barry and Bud Shrake. *Bootlegger's Boy.* New York: Morrow, 1990.

The Texas State Historical Association, the University of Texas Libraries, and the Center for Studies in Texas History. *The Handbook of Texas Online.*

Thomas, Duane and Paul Zimmerman. *Duane Thomas and the Fall of America's Team.* New York: Warner Books, 1988.

Toomay, Pat. *The Crunch.* Lincoln, NE, iUniverse, Inc., 2001.

Magazines

Sports Illustrated
Quarterback
Dallas Cowboy official game programs
Dallas Life Magazine (The Dallas Morning News)
Dave Campbell's Texas Football Magazine
New York
Scene Magazine (The Dallas Morning News)
Sport Magazine
Sport Folio Southwest
Sports Today
Texas Sports
Texas Sportsworld
D Magazine
Texas Monthly

Newspapers

The Dallas Morning News
Dallas Times Herald
Fort Worth Star-Telegram
Herald Democrat, Sherman-Denison
New York Daily News
Dallas Cowboys Official Weekly
The Sporting News
USA Today

Websites

www.wikipedia.org
www.tsha.utexas.edu/handbook/online

INDEX

PEOPLE QUOTED

ABOUT THE AUTHOR

Alan Burton is Director of Public Information at Southeastern Oklahoma State University in Durant, Oklahoma. A native of Sherman, Texas, Burton is a 1979 graduate of Texas Tech University. He has twenty-five years of experience in the field of communications, including newspaper and radio work, and eleven years as the Community Relations Officer for the Sherman Independent School District. He is the author of three other books about Texas:

'til the fat lady sings'—*Classic Texas Sports Quotes*
'rave on'—*Classic Texas Music Quotes*
Texas High School Hotshots—The Stars Before They Were Stars

Popular Texas titles from State House Press

ISBN 1-933337-04-4
$16.95 paper

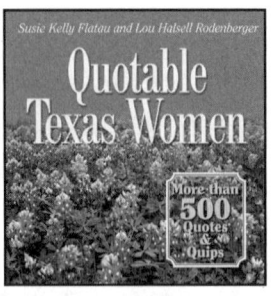

ISBN 1-880510-89-8
$12.95 paper

ISBN 1-880510-83-9
$19.95 cloth

ISBN 1-880510-94-4
$14.95 paper

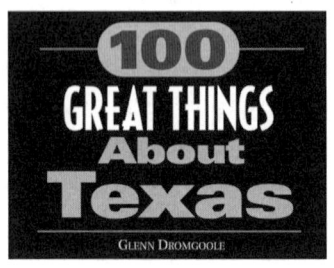

ISBN 1-880510-96-0
$6.95 paper

ISBN 1-880510-87-1
$16.95 paper

ISBN 0-938349-07-4
$14.95 paper

ISBN 1-933337-06-0
$14.95 hardcover w/CD

ISBN 1-880510-80-4
$24.95 cloth

These books available at booksellers or through
Texas A&M University Press Consortium at
1-800-826-8911 or on-line at www.tamu.edu/upress